THE IMPACT OF NEGRO VOTING

AMERICAN POLITICS RESEARCH SERIES

THE IMPACT
OF NEGRO VOTING

The Role of the Vote in the Quest for Equality

William R. Keech
UNIVERSITY OF NORTH CAROLINA
AT CHAPEL HILL

RAND McNALLY & COMPANY • Chicago

AMERICAN POLITICS RESEARCH SERIES
Aaron Wildavsky, Series Editor

For
S. B. K.

45951

PREFACE

Arguments that democracy has failed to provide equal life chances for southern Negroes can be countered by arguments that it has scarcely been tried. Up until recent years, the South has not been a democracy in racial matters for the simple reason that Negroes were for the most part denied the right to vote. Lately, however, this disenfranchisement has been widely eliminated. In this sense the American South in the last decade is a much better test of the ability of democracy to provide equal life chances than is the earlier South. This book evaluates what happens when democracy is tried. The conclusions, then are both about the American race problem and about democracy itself.

The initial stimulus for the book was a conversation with a friend who wasn't sure it is a good idea for Negroes to vote. Among my counter-arguments was one to the effect that Negroes are mistreated less when they vote than when they do not. Having that uneasy feeling of arguing more from conviction than evidence, I checked on what the political science literature had to say on the topic, and found it wanting. This book is the result of my own direct investigation of the subject.

My anticipation by the time I started was that expected payoffs were largely overestimated, but the results of my first preliminary investigations in rural "southside" Virginia were so discouraging that they could have been reported in a short letter to an editor, rather than an article or a book. Concrete payoffs were virtually nil. The settings for this investigation reflect the necessity to study the problem in situations which are more promising for Negro votes.

While the limited payoffs were even more limited than I expected, the most striking addition to my personal education was the recognition of the overwhelming complexity of the problems of the American Negro and the difficulty of overcoming them even with the full cooperation of politicians or anyone else. We have learned a lot since the Watts riots in 1965. In 1967, the incumbent mayor of Durham responded to his loss of Negro endorsement with the slogan "Fairness has not been enough." The sad fact is that there is more truth in his statement than his obvious irony recognizes. It is very late in American racial history. We are still learning that fairness now is not enough to eliminate the effects of unfairness in the past.

ACKNOWLEDGMENTS

Like most books, this one was not written alone. I am indebted to many citizens of Durham and Tuskegee for their time and patience in answering my questions. Without their cooperation the book would literally not have been possible. Robert Lineberry checked most of my calculations on voting patterns in Durham and accompanied me to Tuskegee, where he assisted in all phases of data collection and also contributed his own insightful reactions to the situation there. Linda Crew typed an earlier version and Linda Beam the final manuscript, each with great skill, dispatch and good humor. The University of North Carolina has provided all of the financial support for the project, and its Institute for Research in Social Science provided a reduced teaching load and typing assistance.

Of the several people who have read the manuscript, the following deserve special thanks. Austin Ranney helped translate some crude efforts at analysis into an acceptable dissertation on the Durham situation and provided encouragement when it was most needed. Allan Sindler pointed up errors of fact, logic and emphasis, and generously made his own materials on Durham available to me. Aaron Wildavsky made the kinds of insightful suggestions that one hopes for from an editor. Donald Matthews helped improve the final draft with incisive comments on style and substance. While my wife, Sharon, did not speed the completion of the project, her distractions were welcome. She did make important contributions by being interested and sympathetic, and by expert editorial criticism. I, of course, am solely responsible for the final product.

William R. Keech

Leaksville, North Carolina
August, 1967

Table of Contents

List of Tables

List of Figures

CHAPTER I

Civil Rights, Democratic Theory and Political Science

IN COMMEMORATING THE passage of the Voting Rights Act of 1965, President Johnson observed that "the vote is the most powerful instrument ever devised by man for breaking down injustice and destroying the terrible walls that imprison men because they are different from other men."[1] Yet in a rural Virginia black belt county I visited in 1964, Negroes had constituted over 15 percent of the registered voters for ten years, but the county remained the same segregated, white dominated society it had always been. There were virtually no identifiable payoffs to the Negroes for voting. The President may indulge in a little rhetorical exaggeration in applauding the passage of an act he had strongly favored, but the absence of payoffs under some circumstances does not necessarily mean that gains from voting will be negligible everywhere. The truth would seem to lie somewhere in between the President's assertion and the lack of results in one county. The concern of this book is to determine just where in between.

What sort of payoff, then, does the effort to register Negroes have? What impact does voting have on Negro social and economic status? What concrete advantages result? Does Negro voting bear out the hopes of so many Negroes and the fears of so many whites? Does the vote have an influence over the distribution of advantages that is separate from the influence of those social, economic and political factors that are associated with Negroes getting the vote in the first place?

The research project reported in this book is addressed to these questions. It is meant to shed light on three more or less discrete topics: the prospects that success in voter registration drives will actually improve the status of Negroes, the empirical underpinnings of democratic theory, and some of the problems of empirical political science.

[1] *Newsweek,* August 16, 1965, p. 15.

THE VOTE, THE CIVIL RIGHTS MOVEMENT AND DEMOCRATIC THEORY

'A voteless people is a hopeless people,' has become a cliche. Great amounts of time and money have been expended by organizations such as CORE, NAACP, SNCC and the Southern Regional Council in an effort to get Negroes registered, on the assumption that their social and economic position will thereby be improved. Three out of the four twentieth-century civil rights acts have been aimed at improving Negro status primarily by attempting to guarantee that eligible colored people will have equal access to the ballot box, and all four have dealt with voting rights in some measure.

The struggle to achieve equal voting rights is often placed in the context of conventional wisdom that frequently serves as democratic theory. For example, the vote is said to be basic to all other rights and "in the final analysis, perhaps the most precious right of all in a democracy is the right to vote. With such a right adequately assured, all other rights are potentially assured."[2] Former Attorney General William P. Rogers once stated that

The right to vote . . . occupies a key position because it provides a means of protecting other rights. When minority groups exercise their franchise more effectively, it almost invariably follows that they achieve a greater measure of other fundamental freedoms.[3]

The Southern Regional Council, administrator of the Voter Education Project, points out that

The VEP supposes that increased political participation is a feasible means of bettering the living conditions of deprived groups. The implicit assumption is that the political process is a primary means by which the benefits of society are distributed. This assumption is, of course, basic to democratic theory.[4]

A southern Negro newspaper asserts that "the vote is still the strongest weapon in a democracy," and that once all eligible Negroes vote, "a majority of the obstacles standing in their way will vanish like snow in a summer's sun."[5]

---

[2] Testimony of Andrew J. Biemiller, U. S., House, Sub-committee No. 5 of the Committee on the Judiciary, *Hearings, Civil Rights,* 85th Cong., 1st Sess., 1957, p. 649.
[3] Quoted in Daniel M. Berman, *A Bill Becomes a Law* (New York: Macmillan Co., 1962), pp. 69-70.
[4] "A Statement of the Research Aims and Methods of the Voter Education Project" (Atlanta: Southern Regional Council, February 1963), p. 11. (Mimeographed.)
[5] *Carolina Times* (Durham, N. C.), August 17, 1957 and December 12, 1964.

Such statements are rarely based on systematic empirical research. They are usually calculated to encourage action, but the role of the vote in helping citizens secure concessions from their government must still be one of the crucial questions for the study of democratic politics. There is a need for some sober analysis that will place in sharper relief the prospects that significant improvements in Negro status will result from voting.

While these questions are obviously relevant to the strategy and tactics of the civil rights movement, they are also important in terms of democratic theory itself. The vote is important, not simply because it is one means available to the Negro to improve his social status but also from a more general point of view.

The vote merits attention because it is one of the most widely distributed of all political resources, because all decisions in a democratic form of government rest ultimately on votes, and because it is perhaps the major mechanism for translating popular preferences into governmental decisions. Various groups, from the propertyless to women, have sought the vote on the grounds that it is an important resource in the implementation of their preferences and the recognition of their interests, as well as their worth as persons. The Negro struggle for political rights fits into this same context.

While voting does have an impact on public policy, all too little is known about its nature and limits as a political resource. Marx spoke of the "old democratic litany,"[6] and Lenin claimed that democracy as it is manifest in capitalist society, under conditions most favorable to its development, "is always bound by the narrow framework of capitalist exploitation, and consequently always remains, in reality, a democracy for the minority."[7] To the Marxist, representative democracy does not get to the real conflicts in society.

But do we know that the vote *does* get to the "real conflicts"? Are there prerequisite conditions of a democratic order other than the wide distribution of the vote that must be met before voting becomes an effective resource for deprived groups? Our election system performs two functions: implementing social cleavages and muting them.[8] Perhaps the second overpowers the first.

[6] Karl Marx, "Critique of the Gotha Program," in Lewis S. Feuer (ed.), *Karl Marx and Friedrich Engels, Basic Writings on Politics and Philosophy* (Garden City, N. Y.: Doubleday and Co., Inc., 1959), p. 128.

[7] V. I. Lenin, *State and Revolution* (New York: International Publishers, 1932), pp. 71-72.

[8] See Bernard R. Berelson, Paul F. Lazarsfeld and William N. McPhee, *Voting* (Chicago: University of Chicago Press, 1954), ch. 14, and Talcott Parsons,

What limitations are there on the way the democratic process organizes and implements political conflict? Democracy is on occasion discussed as if it were a mechanism which automatically insured that the interests of all those voting will be attended to by means of some Rousseauian magic. How far is this so?

Murray Edelman has pointed out that when organization is weak and information scarce, the concrete demands for regulation of business are often unwittingly forgotten by deprived groups after they have achieved a change in policy in the form of the passage of a law. The symbols become an effective substitute for the reality of regulation, causing "political quiescence."[9] There may be a parallel in voting. Voting, the symbol of political influence, may be mistaken for the reality.[10] We know too little about how the mechanisms of the policy process shape the impact of the vote.

Obviously there are many factors that may intervene between the ballot box and the outputs of government to affect the impact of the vote. Whether one accepts Marxist ideas like false consciousness or not, it is clear that there are many ways in which individuals can view their own interests and in which they can act on their perceptions.[11] Candidates for public office can define issues and present alternatives (or fail to do so) in many ways.[12] There are also variations in the way in which the political culture may define what is or is not legitimate,[13] and in which the structure of political institutions[14] and the

---

" 'Voting' and the Equilibrium of the American Political System," in Eugene Burdick and Arthur J. Brodbeck (eds.), *American Voting Behavior* (Glencoe, Ill.: The Free Press, 1959), pp. 80-121.

[9] Murray Edelman, "Symbols and Political Quiescence," *American Political Science Review,* LIV (1960), pp. 695-704.

[10] This is not to disparage the symbolic and psychological importance of the vote. On this point see Allan Sindler, "Protest against the Political Status of the Negro," *The Annals of the American Academy of Political and Social Science,* CCCLVII (1965), pp. 48-54.

[11] For a very enlightening discussion of this phenomenon in the context of American businessmen's attitudes on foreign trade, see Raymond A. Bauer, Ithiel de Sola Pool and Lewis A. Dexter, *American Business and Public Policy* (New York: Atherton Press, 1964), ch. 9, Appendix to pt. II, and pt. III.

[12] See E. E. Schattschneider, *The Semisovereign People* (New York: Holt, Rinehart and Winston, 1960).

[13] See Robert E. Agger, Daniel Goldrich and Bert E. Swanson, *The Rulers and the Ruled* (New York: John Wiley and Sons, Inc., 1964), chs. 1-3 and *passim,* and Edward C. Banfield and James Q. Wilson, *City Politics* (Cambridge: Harvard University Press, 1965), pt. III.

[14] See Peter H. Rossi, "Power and Community Structure," *Midwest Journal of Political Science,* IV (1960), pp. 390-400.

realities of bureaucratic power[15] may have an impact on the implementation of preferences expressed at the polls. The research reported here will point out the influence of some of these factors on Negro voting power in two southern cities.

While these are all questions that are relevant to normative democratic theory, they are empirical questions that concern political science as well. There are some other questions, more explicitly related to empirical political science, that this project may also illuminate.

THE VOTE AND EMPIRICAL POLITICAL SCIENCE

The study of voting behavior and political participation has become one of the most ·thoroughly investigated and best understood areas in political science. Yet, as the authors of *The American Voter* point out, virtually all of this effort has gone to discover what factors have influenced the vote, and very little to the question of what the vote has influenced.[16] The situation may be viewed in the light of the growing trend to discuss the various aspects of politics in terms of the organizing principle of a *political system,* which encourages a more systematic attempt to trace *inputs,* such as votes to *outputs* and to find out what happens in between.[17] How are demands translated into decisions? More specifically, how do Negro votes affect policies?

A growing body of recent research has systematically related *demands* in the form of public attitudes, interest group activity, and various dimensions of parties and partisanship to the decisions of government. For example, Miller and Stokes, and Cnudde and McCrone use complex statistical models to trace the relationship between constituency attitudes on various issues and their Congressmen's roll call

[15] See Herbert A. Simon, Donald W. Smithburg and Victor A. Thompson, *Public Administration* (New York: Alfred A. Knopf, 1950),pp. 554-55, and Felix A. Nigro, *Modern Public Administration* (New York: Harper and Row, 1965), ch. 21.

[16] Angus Campbell, Philip E. Converse, Warren E. Miller and Donald E. Stokes, *The American Voter* (New York: John Wiley and Sons, Inc., 1960), p. 539. See also V. O. Key, Jr., "The Politically Relevant in Surveys," *Public Opinion Quarterly,* XXIV (1960), pp. 54-61.

[17] See for example David Easton, "An Approach to the Analysis of Political Systems," *World Politics,* IX (1957), pp. 383-400; Gabriel A. Almond and James S. Coleman, *The Politics of the Developing Areas* (Princeton: Princeton University Press, 1960), "Introduction"; Marian D. Irish and James W. Prothro, *The Politics of American Democracy* (3d ed.; Englewood Cliffs, N. J.: Prentice-Hall, Inc., 1965), pp. 5-19; Easton, *A Framework for Political Analysis* (Englewood Cliffs, N. J.: Prentice-Hall, Inc., 1965); and Easton, *A Systems Analysis of Political Life* (New York: John Wiley and Sons, Inc., 1965).

votes.[18] Bauer, Pool and Dexter treat foreign trade policy in terms of the relationship between public opinion and groups on the one hand, and governmental decisions on the other.[19] Thomas Dye has related several dimensions of party competition, Democratic versus Republican control of state governments, voter participation and malapportionment to numerous policy outcomes in the American states.[20] Other relevant works could be cited, but this area of interaction and influence between citizens and their government remains largely uncharted. This project is meant to contribute to this growing body of literature by analyzing the relationship between Negro voting and the outputs of government in two southern cities.

On another plane, political science is concerned with the study of power and influence, usually in terms of formal political institutions and behavior. However, men like C. Wright Mills, Floyd Hunter and the students of community power in general have emphasized that formal political power and social power are not necessarily congruent.[21] The question of just how important formal political power is in the total social system becomes more salient. Easton has defined politics as the "authoritative allocation of values,"[22] which takes us as political scientists to whatever structures and processes affect this allocation.

What is the relationship between influence over formal political institutions through voting and influence over the allocation of values in the community as a whole?[23] Our Constitution defines some of the limits on governmental power on all levels in this country, and state law further defines the powers of local governments. The decisions involved in defining all of these standards are political decisions; they affect the distribution of advantages and disadvantages. Not only constitutions and laws, but also attitudes and norms influence the impact of formal political proceduces on the allocation of values. Certain

[18] Warren E. Miller and Donald E. Stokes, "Constituency Influence in Congress," *American Political Science Review,* LVII (1963), pp. 45-57, and Charles F. Cnudde and Donald J. McCrone, "The Linkage between Constituency Attitudes and Congressional Voting Behavior: A Causal Model," *Ibid.,* LX (1966), pp. 66-72.

[19] *Op. cit.*

[20] *Politics, Economics and the Public* (Chicago: Rand McNally and Co., 1966). See also Richard E. Dawson and James A. Robinson, "Inter-Party Competition, Economic Variables, and Welfare Policies in the American States," *Journal of Politics,* XXV (1963), pp. 265-89.

[21] See Mills, *The Power Elite* (New York: Oxford University Press, 1956), and Hunter, *Community Power Structure* (Chapel Hill: University of North Carolina Press, 1953) for two of the strongest and best known statements of this argument.

[22] Easton, *The Political System* (New York: Alfred A. Knopf, 1953), ch. 5.

[23] See Norton E. Long, "The Local Community as an Ecology of Games," *American Journal of Sociology,* LXIV (1958), 251-61.

things are perceived as being within the legitimate scope of government activity and others are not.[24] Many of the greatest social conflicts of the last hundred years have been bound up with the question of what is or is not within the proper scope of government.

Also, the control of symbols, legitimacy, goods, violence and skill is not monopolized by those who succeed in the formal political process. Sometimes, as in the late nineteenth century, the balance shifts decidedly away from governmental institutions, or as in the 1930's, towards them. How much of social life do political institutions control? Under what circumstances does this control vary? This project is designed to relate the impact of formal political power in the form of votes to other sources of power in two southern cities.

More specifically, this research is designed to explore the following questions: What is the impact of the Negro vote on the outputs of a local political system, and what is the relationship between the vote as a manifestation of formal political power and other forms and sources of social and political power? Most importantly, is the vote able to achieve major social and economic gains for deprived groups?

The Negro vote will be considered as an independent variable, and the outputs of government will be considered as dependent variables. The formal process of politics, the institutions of government, the values and standards of legitimacy among leaders and followers, and nonpolitical sources of power will be considered as intervening and specifying variables.[25]

What, then, is the impact of Negro voting strength? *The American Voter* discusses consequences of voting in terms of the pressures experienced by those in office, the problems of party strategy, and the structure and competition of the party system.[26] This book will deal most explicitly with the first of these three consequences. Considering the vote as an input into the political system, how is the behavior of public officials affected by its mobilization? What are the limits of voting power? How does the vote stack up with other resources?

The question about the impact of voting is sufficiently complex that I cannot hope to answer it in general. I must investigate it in the context of a particular situation where the conditions can be defined most easily. Hopefully a sound analysis of the impact of Negro voting in a narrowly defined situation will constitute some contribution to the problem areas outlined above.

[24] See Agger, *et al., op. cit.,* ch. 1.
[25] See Herbert Hyman, *Survey Design and Analysis* (New York: The Free Press, 1955), chs. 6-7.
[26] *Op. cit.,* ch. 20.

THE RELEVANCE OF THE SOUTHERN NEGRO

While a project on the impact of Negro voting should have some interest in its own right in this era of the civil rights movement, I hope that the research reported here will be able to speak to even more general questions. While the problem of the Negro was the original stimulus for the project, the research was not tied to the Negro as a vehicle for studying the impact of the vote on the fortunes of deprived groups. A project might have been designed to study the impact of gaining the vote on the fortunes of immigrant ethnic groups, property-less and non-taxpaying groups, and even women, all of whom were without the vote at some times or places. The Negro, however, lends himself to a feasible research project somewhat better than do any of the other groups mentioned, for the following reasons.

1. SIZE. Researchers have assumed all along that the impact of the vote on governmental outputs can be studied only by looking at groups of some size relative to the governmental unit in question. Individuals and very small groups have too limited an impact on the overall distribution of values as it is determined by the voting process, although they may have considerable impact through the use of other resources, such as money, skill of various kinds, etc.

While Negroes are not such a large group in the nation as a whole, their number is exaggerated by their concentration in certain areas. They are particularly numerous in the South as a whole and in the large cities of the North. Finding governmental units where Negroes constitute a very large minority or even a majority is not at all difficult.

2. COHESIVE BEHAVIOR. In trying to assess the impact of the votes of a large group of people, the group should ideally vote together so most members do not cancel one another's voting power, but rather act together so as to maximize the group's electoral strength. While a group may not have to vote together to increase its political influence, this would seem to help. Cohesive voting would seem to clarify and simplify the problem.

Negroes are quite cohesive in their voting behavior. As the authors of *The American Voter* point out, the cohesiveness of groups will vary from time to time and place to place according to such factors as level of identification of individuals with the group, the transmission of group political standards, the political salience of the group for its members, the legitimacy of group political activity, and the percent of one's life spent in close contact with the group.[27] While Negroes are subject to variation on all of these factors, Campbell *et al.*

[27] *Ibid.*, ch. 12.

found the Negro community to be the most cohesive of the groups we have surveyed. Furthermore, Negroes, as we shall see, are almost unanimous in their belief that the group has a right to further its ends by political activity.[28]

3. IDENTIFIABLE BEHAVIOR. The group should predominate in easily identifiable sections rather than spread out. This way their voting behavior can be measured by aggregate data analysis, rather than necessitating surveys of some sort to ascertain vote direction and cohesion.

The residential segregation of Negroes makes it unusually easy to identify and measure their behavior. Finding entirely or predominantly Negro precincts in cities that have Negro populations of any size is usually not hard. Thus Negro voting behavior lends itself very well to study by aggregate data analysis.[29]

4. UNIFORM DEPRIVATION AND A WIDE RANGE OF IDENTIFIABLE GOALS ON WHICH THERE IS HIGH AGREEMENT. In trying to measure whether or not a group's goals are achieved, goals must be shared by most members of the group and these goals must be distinguishable in some way either from the status quo, from the goals of the rest of society or both. Otherwise there would be no way of measuring the success or impact of cohesive group voting. The wider the range of such goals, the more dimensions there are on which to measure achievement.

Negroes have probably come as close as any group to having high agreement about identifiable goals because of the many-faceted consequences of segregation. Although there is almost as much variation among Negroes with respect to occupation, education, ability, income, achievement, etc. as in any other group, the badge of color has been the mark of differential treatment unrelated to other, more rational sources of discrimination to a degree not found in any comparable group.

The Negro lawyer or surgeon may have no more in common with his maid than the white lawyer or surgeon has with his; the successful Negro may have everything that talent, ambition and hard work can achieve—but for the lack of equal treatment accorded those with a black skin. The simple factors of segregation and prejudice have made for common interests between the wealthy Negro and the poor, the talented

---

[28] *Ibid.*, p. 316.

[29] This is not necessarily to yield to the "ecological fallacy" pointed out by W. S. Robinson in "Ecological Correlations and the Behavior of Individuals," *American Sociological Review*, XV (1950), pp. 351-57. This analysis will use vote returns in all Negro precincts in Durham to draw inferences about the voting behavior of that group of Negroes living in those precincts. This is safe in this case so long as we do not extend these comments to all Durham Negroes or different types of individual Negroes in the precincts utilized.

Negro and the humble. Over the whole range of Negro stratification, discrimination in jobs, education and public accommodations has made for a high unanimity of grievances. No matter what his station in life, every Negro has an interest in equal treatment.

While there is a high degree of stratification among Negroes, this should not be emphasized to the point of obscuring the fact that most Negroes fall into the lower levels of almost every social grouping. Most Negroes are low in education, income and the other indicators of socio-economic status. This fact reinforces their cohesiveness as a group and adds an economic dimension to racial discrimination.

5. A BASIS FOR COMPARISON. If we are to attempt to draw conclusions about the impact of voting as opposed to nonvoting, or about the utility of the vote in achieving certain social or economic gains, there must be some variation in either or both. For example, there must either be situations where Negroes vote and where they do not, or situations where Negroes have achieved certain gains and where they have not.[30]

Negroes lend themselves well here, also. While disenfranchisement of the Negro was supposedly outlawed by the Fifteenth Amendment, it is still in the process of being finally wiped out. In fact, in most of the states of the Old Confederacy, almost all Negroes were effectively denied the vote until the white primary was outlawed in 1944. Since then, for various reasons, the growth of Negro voting has been slow. Thus there are numerous opportunities in the South to study given areas and compare them both before and after Negroes began voting in large numbers, or to compare areas where Negroes vote with otherwise similar areas where Negroes do not vote.

In 1960 there were numerous counties in the South where no Negroes were registered at all, as well as others where Negro registration reached over 60 percent. There were numerous counties where Negroes constituted 0 percent of county registration, and others where they constituted more than 20 percent, and even two where they made up over half of the registered voters.[31] There is also a great deal of variation in the degree to which Negroes have overcome the disadvantages of discrimination and segregation. There was even more when this project was launched. All of this provides ample material for comparison.

6. AVAILABILITY OF INFORMATION. Studying a more or less contemporary situation is desirable so the information can be collected by

[30] See ch. 2.
[31] U. S., Commission on Civil Rights, *Report,* Vol. I, *Voting* (Washington: U. S. Government Printing Office, 1961), pp. 251-312.

the researcher himself, or the situation should be one about which there is already considerable information available.

Negroes are again the most appropriate group for study. For them the process of political assimilation is still going on. One is not totally dependent on inadequate printed information collected by other persons for other purposes. The researcher is able to investigate the situation himself and to observe it and to talk to participants. This is not possible with any of the other groups. Given the scarcity of information on this problem for any one of them, this is a major advantage, and would probably be controlling if other things were equal.

7. CURRENT IMPORTANCE. If all the possible groups were equally useful for designing a research project of this nature, the Negro would still have the advantage because the Negro revolution is still a public issue and a source of widespread concern and dispute. So, for all these reasons, the Negroes lend themselves to research about the impact of voting on the realization of group goals in a way that no other group does. Thus we turn to the Negro as the most apt vehicle for research on this topic.

Are there any disadvantages to using the Negro as such a vehicle? There seem to be very few, if any. Perhaps one might say that the Negro is an unfair test or too demanding a test of the impact of the vote because of the unpopularity of Negro goals and the complexity of resolving many of the problems of the Negro. Perhaps the obstacles to be overcome by Negro voting are too strong. To this we might reply that given the importance of the vote for democratic theory and the importance of the vote in the activities of the civil rights movement, a demanding test is very much in order.

CHAPTER II

The Setting and the Method

THIS BOOK HAS been written with the conviction that systematic empirical political science can and should address problems of social importance even when they do not lend themselves very well to the most sophisticated techniques modern social sciences offer. The impact of the vote in securing justice for deprived groups is surely one of the more important problems in the study of democratic politics, as the previous chapter argued, yet it does not yield to systematic analysis quite so readily as many more narrowly defined problems. In order to make this a manageable project, I have limited the setting to two southern cities. This chapter will describe those locales and their relevance to the topic, and explain how information about the impact of votes on policy can be derived from a study of these two cities.

THE SETTING

I have chosen to investigate this problem on the local, rather than the state or national level, because it is far more manageable. Identifying and measuring differences, both in Negro voting and also in policy outputs to Negroes, is easier in a smaller and simpler, rather than a larger and more complex locale. Furthermore a city or county is likely to be a homogeneous unit as far as patterns of voting and public policy are concerned. In contrast, a state or the nation involves a multitude of political subunits like cities and counties which are likely to have widely varying degrees of Negro voting and widely varying public policies towards Negroes. Limiting our view to the local level does not prohibit our looking at state or federal policies as they bear on Negroes at the local level. After all, everyone lives at some local level and is affected by state and federal policy. The choice of a local focus simply reflects a desire to use units wherein the necessary data can be collected and wherein the problem can be investigated with a minimum of extraneous complicating factors.

The two units I have chosen are Durham, North Carolina and Tuskegee, Alabama. These two cities share a large number of characteristics and differ in many others, but for our purposes the most important thing they have in common is that they have discriminated against Negroes in the past. Without some discrimination for Negro voting to eliminate, there would be little of import to study. Because of our interest in the effects of voting on fair and equal treatment, I must study places where such fairness has not always been the practice. Unfortunately, finding such locales in the United States—North and South —is all too easy, but southern discrimination has probably been more thorough and wide-ranging (although less subtle) than in the North, and consequently offers a wider range of practices for the vote to eliminate.

That Negroes have not always been able to vote without restriction in Durham and Tuskegee is also an important factor. We can easily find discrimination in the North, but because there has not been substantial disfranchisement of Negroes there, it is not so easy to study the effects of different levels of voting strength. We might investigate the effects of different sizes of Negro electorate, but we would not as a rule be able to study the effects of changes in Negro voting strength in one setting. We would not be able to study what happens when restrictions on the right to vote are removed, as we can in the South. Changes like these are common in the South but almost nonexistent in the North. In the South Negroes are just gaining the vote, and consequently in the South the impact of Negro voting has the greatest interest.

The differences between Durham and Tuskegee are as striking as the similarities. Tuskegee is the county seat of a small, heavily rural Alabama black belt county, while Durham is the fifth largest city in North Carolina.[1] The stereotyped image of the difference between such areas is borne out by relevant census figures. Durham county is 75.6 percent urban, while only 13.3 percent of Macon County residents

[1] In 1960 there were 111,995 persons in Durham County and 78,302 persons in the city of Durham, which has since grown through annexation. Macon County, where Tuskegee is located, had a 1960 population of 26,717. The census lists the population of Tuskegee at 1,750, but this was just before the U. S. Supreme Court held that it was unconstitutional for the state of Alabama to change the shape of the city from a square to a twenty-eight sided figure. The effect of this change was to exclude virtually every Negro voter from the city without excluding any whites. See *Gomillion v. Lightfoot*, 364 U. S. 339 (1960). Current estimates of Tuskegee's population range from 6,700 to 9,000.

13

live in urban places.[2] Durham County's 1960 median family income of $4,876 is just over twice that of Macon County. Just under a third of Durham County's population is Negro, while over four-fifths of Macon's is nonwhite.[3] Only 2.4 percent of Durham County's employed labor force is in agriculture, while 21.4 percent of Macon's workers earn their money in farming. Durham County lost only 6.5 percent of its population through migration between 1950 and 1960 while Macon lost 26.9 percent!

Thus on these measures, Tuskegee represents the 'traditional' South with its agricultural economy and heavy Negro population. Durham, part of the industrial Piedmont crescent stretching from Raleigh into South Carolina, approximates the 'new South' with its belching smoke-stacks. The visual aspect of the two cities is appropriate. Tuskegee centers on the inevitable courthouse square with its monument to local Confederate dead. The ante-bellum and Victorian mansions are there too, often in some stage of decay. Durham has a much different appearance. While Tuskegee is still sleepy enough to have angle parking with plenty of vacant spaces in the central square, Durham's crowded center is a busy business district just beginning the process of urban renewal. The contrasts are sharp between the modern and the dated storefronts in the central business district. Nearby are the tobacco and textile factories that are among the city's largest employers, and the high rise office buildings of insurance companies and banks.

In these respects Durham and Tuskegee would seem almost identical to many other mid-South industrial cities and small black belt cities, respectively. They are not, however, and it is in their Negro communities that they contrast most sharply with their counterparts. Both of these cities have some unusual Negro institutions that give them a very sizeable Negro business and professional elite, which serves as an important leadership base. These elites will have an important bearing on the political problems I will analyze.

Both cities have Negro colleges, which employ large numbers of Negro academic and administrative personnel. North Carolina College is a state liberal arts college whose students are almost entirely Negro. Tuskegee Institute is the college made famous by Booker T. Washington and George Washington Carver.

Tuskegee is also the site of a large Veterans' Administration Hos-

---

[2] This figure is likely to be somewhat misleading for Tuskegee, given the gerrymander. Indeed 13.3 percent of the total population of the county is 3,553—about half of the current estimates for Tuskegee. The point is that the Tuskegee area is a much less urbanized area than Durham.

[3] The city of Durham is 36.3 percent Negro, while estimates place Tuskegee's Negro population between 72 and 82 percent.

pital which was formerly staffed entirely by Negroes, and still has Negroes on all levels of employment all the way up to the director himself. Durham is the home of an insurance company that is called the largest Negro-owned business in the U. S. Its new, modern home is Durham's tallest structure. A Negro bank and a savings and loan association are also important sources of Negro leadership.

Still, these cities are even more unusual than is directly apparent from their substantial Negro middle class. Negroes in Durham and Tuskegee have achieved a strength at the polls that sets them apart in all of the South. As the next chapter will show in detail, Tuskegee has achieved voting strength in terms of percent of the electorate Negro that is probably not matched anywhere in the United States. Durham Negroes have developed a bloc of votes that is probably unmatched in cohesiveness and maneuverability. Clearly these cities were not chosen because they are typical settings for Negroes in politics. Each city also has a remarkable Negro organization that is largely responsible for its Negro voting strength. The Tuskegee Civic Association is a blanket organization which takes an interest in general Negro affairs. A related unit, the Macon County Democratic Club, takes care of political matters, such as endorsement of candidates. The Durham Committee on Negro Affairs endorses candidates in Durham elections and turns out the vote for the endorsee. Because the voting strength and leadership of Negroes are so important to this study I will pay considerably more attention to each. The next chapter will be devoted to the Negro vote, and leadership will be brought in at some length in succeeding chapters.

In anticipation of that, however, I may point out now that Negro leaders in both cities are excellent cases of what Matthews and Prothro called "moderate" as opposed to "militant" or "traditional" Negro leadership, in that their socioeconomic status is high, and they are economically independent of whites. Further, their goals center on general improvement of welfare of all Negroes through gradual change. Most importantly, their tactics involve continuous, overt and organized efforts at litigation and bargaining, while their major resources are control over votes and legal challenges.[4]

A word should be added about the formal political structure of the two cities. The chief administrative official in Tuskegee is the elected mayor, while Durham is a city manager city. Each city is non-partisan. Tuskegee elects its part-time mayor for two years and its twelve councilmen for simultaneous four year terms, while the terms of Durham councilmen overlap.

[4] See Donald R. Matthews and James W. Prothro, *Negroes and the New Southern Politics* (New York: Harcourt, Brace and World, Inc., 1966), pp. 195-200.

In both cities the candidates are elected by all of the city's voters, rather than wards, but there are complications in Durham. There is a councilman representing and living in each of six wards in Durham, although he is elected by the voters of all wards. Six councilmen are elected at large. Three of the ward and three of the at-large councilmen are chosen every two years.

Because the ward candidates in Durham are elected by all the voters, Negro candidates must depend on white as well as Negro votes for election, even though there is one virtually all Negro ward. In practice in recent years, however, there is virtually no white competition for the third ward seat. The main reasons for this are probably that there are virtually no whites living there, and that this seat seems to be viewed as the Negro seat on the council.[5]

Why were Durham and Tuskegee chosen for this study, rather than two other communities? The answer is derived from my interest in findings with a maximum import for general knowledge about the impact of Negro voting on policy. Obviously we cannot generalize from two cases, which are not a sample of anything. As my description of them indicates they were not even randomly selected.

The choice is the result of a research strategy that was based in part on a hypothesis and in part on some preliminary research. Insofar as such an exploratory study as this was initially guided by specific hypotheses, the major one was that the impact of the Negro vote has been widely overestimated and that its impact would be limited and subtle. The first empirical investigation was in a rural 'southside' Virginia county where Negro voting had risen from 2 to 22 percent of the electorate in a period of twenty years. The major findings of that study became clear very quickly: even such an increase in Negro voting had not had any noticeable impact on life for Negroes there.

The resulting strategy for the remainder of the project was to find

[5] For further treatment of Tuskegee, see Bernard Taper, *Gomillion versus Lightfoot* (New York: McGraw-Hill Co., Inc., 1962); Lewis Jones and Stanley Smith, *Tuskegee, Alabama: Voting Rights and Economic Pressure* (New York: Anti-Defamation League of B'nai B'rith, 1958); and Woodrow Wadsworth Hall, *A Bibliography of the Tuskegee Gerrymander Protest* (Tuskegee Institute, Alabama: Department of Records and Research, 1960). More materials on Durham can be found in R. Lewis Bowman, "Negro Politics in Four Southern Counties" (Ph.D. dissertation, University of North Carolina, 1963); Bradbury Seasholes and Frederic N. Cleaveland, "Negro Political Participation in Two Piedmont Crescent Cities," in F. Stuart Chapin, Jr., and Shirley F. Weiss, eds., *Urban Growth Dynamics* (New York: John Wiley and Sons, 1962), pp. 260-308; Allan P. Sindler, *Negro Protest and Local Politics in Durham, N. C.* (Eagleton Institute Cases in Practical Politics, No. 37, 1965); and Harry J. Walker, "Changes in Race Accommodation in a Southern Community" (Ph.D. dissertation, University of Chicago, 1945).

some units where Negro voting had reached such a level that it would have some identifiable impact that could be studied. This meant finding communities with even larger and stronger Negro electorates. Tuskegee has recently become a city with a majority of its electorate Negro, and allows us to see what happens as a result of voting under apparently optimum conditions. The Negro vote there is so large that it could achieve little more in other settings than it brings in Tuskegee. Durham Negroes constitute a more moderate, but still unusually high proportion of their electorate. In 1960, 88 percent of southern counties for which full Negro voter registration data was available had smaller proportions of their electorate Negro.[6] In those counties we would expect, other things being equal, that the payoffs of Negro voting would be generally less than those in Durham. The payoffs in Durham are limited enough to make that an important statement. After the Voting Rights Act of 1965 has had its full impact, Durham will no doubt move towards the mean, but probably still remain unusual in the cohesion and maneuverability of its voting bloc.

The strategy for approaching generalization can be expressed as follows. In Tuskegee I demonstrate the substantial impact of a Negro voting majority. With Durham I move to a somewhat more ordinary percentage of the electorate Negro, but one which is directed in elections with extraordinary efficiency. I find the payoffs from elections to be far less than in Tuskegee. Because the overwhelming bulk of southern communities has a proportionately smaller Negro electorate and a less cohesive and maneuverable bloc vote, we expect the impact of the vote to be even less than in Durham in those counties. While this is a weak kind of generalization, it is a substantial payoff from a study of two communities.

The generalization is not without assumptions. The basic assumption is that the relationship between voting strength and policy outputs is positive and more or less linear, i.e., other things being equal, each increment in Negro voting strength will bring with it an increment in favorable policy outputs.

[6] U. S., Commission on Civil Rights, *Report,* Vol. I, *Voting* (Washington: U. S. Government Printing Office, 1961), pp. 252-312. Actually Durham County's electorate was 22.2 percent Negro, and 88 percent of the counties in the eleven states of the Confederacy for which such information was available had less than 20 percent. The distribution was

0— 9.9% of electorate Negro	64%
10—19.9	24
20—29.9	9
30—39.9	2
40 and over	1
	100%

But what impact does the 'other things being equal' assumption have? If 88 percent of southern counties were below Durham in percent of the electorate Negro, but only 30 percent were below it in some other relevant characteristic such as quality of Negro leadership my 'generalization' would be less valid. Fortunately I am not without an independent judgment on this matter. Donald Matthews and James Prothro rank Negro leadership in four very different southern communities on their success in instilling morale in their followers and maintaining wide consent to rule, and in their effectiveness in attaining group goals. Their "Piedmont County," which is almost certainly Durham, ranks first among their four counties on both counts.[7]

If Durham is not too much less unusually high in the quality of its Negro leadership than it is in the strength of its Negro vote, I can be relatively confident in the generalization that in counties with weaker Negro votes the payoffs from voting will be generally no greater than in Durham.

This attempt at generalization must not be taken *too* seriously. I will argue later that the relationship between Negro votes and payoffs may be slightly curvilinear rather than linear. Also the impact of the Voting Rights Act of 1965 may place more and more counties above Durham in Negro voting strength. The point is that as far as we know, there is reason to expect fewer, rather than more, payoffs from Negro voting in many other southern communities than we find in these two.

THE RESEARCH DESIGN[8]

In trying to assess the impact of Negro voting on public policy towards Negroes, the problem is to investigate a causal relationship between votes, the independent or causing variable, and public policy, the dependent variable. While we recognize that virtually all social phenomena—and surely public policy—have multiple causes, our interest is predominantly in only one of the independent variables that influence public policy—Negro votes. Thus our focus will be on a two variable relationship. I will consider other independent variables, but mainly to clarify the role that Negro voting plays in determining outcomes.

There are numerous alternative methods of generating information about causal relationships, the most basic of which are laboratory experiments and survey analysis. In the former, the experimenter conducts

[7] *Loc. cit.*

[8] The remainder of this chapter is of interest primarily to the methodologically oriented social scientist. While it is expendable for the general reader, I hope that it will be enlightening to him about problems of generating causal inferences on topics such as this.

his research in an artificial laboratory, which he uses to hold some variables constant and to vary others. In the latter, the investigator gathers information on a large number of cases and uses statistical methods to assess the relationship between variables. Unfortunately neither of these techniques is practically available for investigation of this problem.

The laboratory experiment is out of the question because the smallest unit whose outputs could be linked to Negro votes is the community, and recreating relevant aspects of a community in a laboratory, or experimentally manipulating the level or degree of Negro voting is not possible. The survey analysis is much more feasible, but the problem here is a lack of available information. Identifying differences in Negro voting strength among, for example, all counties in the South, and relating them to differences in public policy outputs in those counties would be quite useful. The Civil Rights Commission has identified the percentage of Negroes registered and the percent of the electorate Negro in almost all southern counties. The problem is the availability of information on the dependent variable. There is very limited information available on a county basis about what kinds of benefits Negroes may have received as a result of voting.[9]

Such information, if it is to be at all inclusive of potential payoffs from voting, must be collected by the investigator himself. This limits the study to the number of cases that there are time, money and personnel to study. Assuming that the number is too low for the use of statistical methods of analysis, the nature of the study must be changed somewhat to a natural experiment or an *ex post facto* study. This could take the form of a study of one community over a period of time that ranges from no or very limited Negro voting to a more substantial level of political participation. Alternatively it could take the form of a study of two or more communities at the same point in time, but varying in the level of Negro voting.[10]

[9] Most useful are the statistical summaries of school desegregation published by the Southern Educational Reporting Service of Nashville, Tennessee. It is apparent, however, that litigation and Federal guidelines have had more to do with school desegregation than voting has.

[10] Donald T. Campbell and Julian C. Stanley would call this a "pre-experimental design." See their *Experimental and Quasi-Experimental Designs for Research* (Chicago: Rand McNally and Co., 1963), pp. 7-13. For other examples of this type of research, see Leon D. Epstein, "A Comparative Study of Canadian Parties," *American Political Science Review*, LVIII (1964), pp. 46-60; Edwin H. Rhyne, "Political Parties and Decision Making in Three Southern Counties," *Ibid.*, LII (1958), 1091-108; Robert E. Lane, "The Politics of Consensus in an Age of Affluence," *Ibid.*, LIX (1965), pp. 874-95; and Bernard E. Brown, "Pressure Politics in the Fifth Republic," *Journal of Politics*, XXV (1963), pp. 509-25. The first two utilize a spatial comparison and the second two a longitudinal comparison.

This project will take both forms. Two communities are studied, which gives it the form of a spatial comparison of two units at similar points in time, but each community is studied longitudinally as well. I have thus investigated the effects of changes in Negro voting strength over time as well as the effects of differences in such strength between the cities.

Each of the letters a, b, c, d in Figure II-1 represents a juxta-position of the level or degree of Negro voting strength at a specified time and place, and public policy outputs for Negroes at that point. Thus comparisons a–c and b–d will show the effects on policy of changes in Negro voting strength in one city over time. Comparisons a–b and c–d will show the effects on policy of differences in voting strength *between* cities at *one* point in time. Comparing a–x and x–y or combinations of other points is also possible.

FIGURE II–1
Level of Negro Voting Strength

	Durham	Tuskegee
Time 1	a	b
Time 2	c	d
Time N	x	y

Because of limitations in the data that can be generated, I will not be able to make all of the comparisons that are possible in principle, but the two cities will yield enough information to permit me to identify concomitant variation in the independent and dependent variables, the *sine qua non* of causal inference. The nature and limitations of the data will be discussed below.

Besides demonstrating concomitant variation, I must also deal with problems of time order and spuriousness in order to make sound causal inferences. The problem of demonstrating that a change in policy towards Negroes is preceded rather than followed by a change in voting strength will be dealt with by emphasizing the comparisons between times in each city. Thus I will be able to observe the time sequences by looking at the value of the dependent variable both before and after a change in the independent variable. This is not possible when one is simply comparing cities at one point in time.[11]

[11] See Hans L. Zetterburg, *On Theory and Verification in Sociology,* 3rd ed.

One of the major difficulties of such studies as these is the difficulty of controlling the possible impact of other variables which may cause spurious associations between votes and policy. As Gunnar Myrdal has pointed out,

It is hard to demonstrate that a given number of Negro votes will procure a given amount of legal justice for Negroes, because it can be claimed, and correctly so, that those communities which allow Negroes to vote to a given extent will also usually be willing to give them other legal rights to a comparable extent.[12]

Even if we find Negro voting associated with Negro enjoyment of favorable public policy outputs, the same factors which cause Negro voting may independently cause the benefits we may be inclined to attribute to the vote. The vote may add little or nothing to the likelihood that Negroes will enjoy certain benefits that are really the result of the same factors that brought about voting itself. For example, Matthews and Prothro have found that the same twenty-one social and economic factors that explain about 28 percent of the variation in Negro registration ($R = .53$) explain about 25 percent of the variation in school desegregation in the South ($R = .50$).[13] While an association may be found between voting and school desegregation, the variation in school desegregation might be accounted for by the factors that explain voting and not by voting itself. Because so little is known about the factors that cause equal treatment and favorable public policy for Negroes, I anticipate that communities differing in the strength of their Negro vote may differ on so many other variables that might be related to policy that being sure it is the vote and not the other characteristics that is causing any difference in public policy outputs is difficult. Thus, some way of separating the influence of voting from that of other factors that may be associated with the independent and dependent variables must be found.

A relationship may be spurious whether it be demonstrated over

---

(Totowa, N. J.: The Bedminster Press, 1965), p. 135 for further comments on the advantages of a longitudinal design. It is true that the longitudinal design in this case makes us especially susceptible to "history" and "maturation" as sources of internal invalidity. See Campbell and Stanley, *op. cit.*, pp. 7-9. I will deal with this problem below.

[12] Gunnar Myrdal, *An American Dilemma* (New York: Harper and Row, 1944), p. 497.

[13] See Donald R. Matthews and James W. Prothro, "Social and Economic Factors and Negro Voter Registration in the South," *American Political Science Review*, LVII (1963), p. 42; and Matthews and Prothro, "Stateways versus Folkways: Critical Factors in Southern Reaction to Brown v. Board of Education," in Gottfried Dietze (ed.), *Essays on the American Constitution* (Englewood Cliffs, N. J.: Prentice-Hall, Inc., 1964), p. 149.

time or between units, and no amount of controls can put a relationship totally beyond question. Still, some relationships are demonstrated more convincingly than others. My strategy must be to make the causal arguments as convincing as possible. An argument that Negro votes affect policy that is based on a comparison between communities may be rendered valueless by the fact that there are other important differences between the communities which account for the difference in policy. Similarly such an argument based on change in Negro votes over time may be rendered valueless by other factors changing over time. Because I do not have the opportunity to use sophisticated statistical controls, I must be careful to base my arguments on comparisons that involve the least risks of unfounded causal inference.

The tremendous variability of communities makes it very difficult to match them with much confidence that they are similar in relevant respects other than the independent and dependent variables. Durham and Tuskegee are almost as different as two southern communities can be anyway. The longitudinal study is a way of avoiding this problem when it is not possible to introduce statistical controls. When the investigator looks at one community at differing points in time, he is in effect holding the community constant. This is not foolproof, of course, because other relevant community characteristics may change over time with the independent variable.[14] Still, it may be easier to keep track of the other variables if the setting remains constant. If the changes in the independent and dependent variables occur relatively abruptly and simultaneously, the problem of spuriousness is less serious than it is when the independent variable changes very slowly and gradually and the results are also slow in coming. The changes were abrupt in Tuskegee and gradual in Durham.

While the slowness of the changes in Durham and the sharpness of the distinctions between the two cities make inferences based on such comparisons tenuous, the change over time in Tuskegee was so abrupt and striking as to allow very convincing inferences. Such will be the argument. The strongest positive causal inferences will be based on the longitudinal study in Tuskegee. In Durham, I will argue that the vote did not have such a striking effect. This argument will be based on observations that certain policies were not achieved at all, and that some were as clearly attributable to factors other than voting as policies in Tuskegee were to voting. I have already indicated that the theme will emphasize what voting does *not* achieve even in situations as auspicious as Durham.

There are other more constructive ways besides spurious correla-

---

[14] See Campbell and Stanley, *op. cit.,* pp. 7-9.

tions in which third variables may tie into the relationship between votes and policy. These are what Herbert Hyman calls interpretation and specification.[15] Interpretation involves a developmental sequence through which the independent variable affects the dependent variable. A third variable intervenes without rendering the initial relationship spurious. It *interprets* it by demonstrating the process through which the initial independent variable affects the dependent variable. For example, constituency attitudes may affect Congressional roll call votes through a process involving the Congressman's own attitudes or through a process involving his perception of constituency preferences.[16]

While I will not be able to use quantitative techniques to demonstrate such developmental sequences, I will be able to shed some light on them. When it can be demonstrated that the vote did cause a change in policy, I can often point out the process through which the change occurred. For example, if a policy decision was made through a bond issue election, and Negro votes provided the margin of victory of the bond issue, I may reasonably conclude that Negro votes affected the outcome through the process of bond issue elections. Alternatively they may affect the outcome through determining the election of more favorable public officials, or perhaps through changing the values and issue preferences of existing public officials. The method in doing this will basically be one of pointing out what happened when votes can be linked to a change in policy.

Specification involves looking at the strength of a relationship under differing underlying conditions. For example, the relationship between party identification and voting behavior is stronger among people with poorly developed attitudes than among those with well developed attitudes.[17] Similarly the relationship between votes and policy may be stronger in communities with a sympathetic white population than it is where the whites are uniformly hostile to Negro demands. Here again the data provide a limited opportunity for such analysis. I will hypothesize that some of the differences in payoffs between Durham and Tuskegee can be accounted for in part by differences between the two cities other than Negro voting. For example white resistance to Negro gains may help account for why a given proportion of votes brought fewer gains in one city than the other.

[15] *Survey Design and Analysis* (New York: Free Press, 1955), ch. 6-7.
[16] See Warren E. Miller and Donald E. Stokes, "Constituency Influence in Congress," *American Political Science Review*, LVII (1963), pp. 355-67; and Charles F. Cnudde and Donald J. McCrone, "The Linkage between Constituency Attitudes and Congressional Voting Behavior: A Causal Model," *Ibid.*, LX (1966), pp. 66-72.
[17] Angus Campbell, Philip E. Converse, Warren E. Miller and Donald E. Stokes, *The American Voter* (New York: John Wiley, 1960), pp. 141-42.

CHAPTER III

Negro Voting Strength in Two Cities

DURHAM AND TUSKEGEE are both cities with remarkably strong Negro votes, but their strengths are manifested in very different ways. Tuskegee Negroes have a strength of numbers that Durham Negroes can never hope to approach simply because Durham does not contain a high enough proportion of Negro residents. On the other hand, Durham Negroes have reached a technical efficiency in mobilizing a moderately sized electorate that would be the envy of interest group leaders anywhere. This chapter will analyze several dimensions of Negro voting in the two cities. Because of limitations of available data, the Tuskegee account will be limited to data on Negro registration, while data on Durham will permit more elaborate analyses that include other dimensions of voting strength. Fortunately this will not hinder the overall analysis of the impact of Negro voting because the size of the registered Negro electorate, rather than the other dimensions, is important in Tuskegee.

THE REGISTRATION OF NEGRO VOTERS

Most of the discussion, legislation, litigation and direct action that has been directed toward the problem of Negro political participation has, with justification, been concerned with voter registration. Just as white Southerners have devoted so much of their efforts to perfecting literacy tests, poll taxes and related forms of discrimination and intimidation at the registration stage, most of the efforts of the federal government and the civil rights movement in the voting area have been designed to protect the right of the Negro to register. This is reasonable enough on both sides because registration is the first step in participating in the electoral process, and because it has long been a sticking point at which such participation has been curtailed or prohibited. Registration is the *sine qua non* of voting.

The story of the fight for the unrestricted right to vote in Tuskegee is a well known and highly dramatic one. Tuskegee was ingenious enough to reduce itself from a large rectangle to a small twenty-eight sided figure resembling a stylized sea horse in order to exclude virtually all Negroes from its borders and its electorate. Tuskegee Negroes took this case all the way to the United States Supreme Court to secure the protection of their right to vote.

This story is well told elsewhere,[1] but for our purpose it is retold by the figures in Table III-1, which reports the increase in the absolute and relative size of the Negro electorate in Beat One of Macon County, which includes Tuskegee. As many as thirty-two Negroes were registered by 1928, and seventy-seven by 1940, but in 1941 Tuskegee Negroes began their efforts to register in large numbers with the reorganization of the Tuskegee's Men's Club as the Tuskegee Civic Association, which made registration one of its primary objectives. As early as 1943 a threat of legal action against the Board of Registrars secured removal of the limitation on which registered voters were permitted to vouch for applicants. Up until the late thirties, the Board had required that the character of each applicant be "vouched for" by white registered voters, but after that a handful of 'selected' Negro voters was recognized as acceptable vouchers. The first actual litigation against the Board of Registrars was brought in 1945, and Tuskegee Negroes had been in and out of court from then until the fruition of their efforts in the United States Supreme Court's *Gomillion v. Lightfoot* decision of 1960.[2]

Tuskegee's problems in maintaining a white electorate had been receiving the direct attention of Alabama's governors, legislature and supreme court for years, but after 1954, the year of *Brown v. Board of Education* and the year that the first Negro ran for public office in Macon County, efforts were more strongly mobilized. In 1955 Macon's state senator announced plans to introduce a bill to abolish the county if the U. S. Supreme Court attempted to enforce school desegregation and if a working board of registrars (one that would not be dilatory, discriminate, or resign to avoid registering Negroes) were appointed in

[1] See Bernard Taper, *Gomillion versus Lightfoot* (New York: McGraw-Hill Book Co., Inc., 1962); and Lewis Jones and Stanley Smith, *Voting Rights and Economic Pressure* (New York: Anti-Defamation League of B'nai B'rith, 1958).
[2] 364 U. S. 399 (1960).

the county. Such a bill was later introduced, but ultimately foundered because of the unwillingness of any of the adjoining counties to take Tuskegee![3]

TABLE III–1

Negro Registration in Beat One, Macon County[a]

Year	Total Registration	Total Negro Registration	Percent of Reg- istered Voters Negro
1952	1612	589	36.6%
1954	2056	810	39.4
1956	2218	1006	45.3
1958	2201	947	43.0
1960	2296	1060	46.6
1962	3535	2151	60.8
1964	4584	3077	67.1
1966	6962	4914	70.5

[a] Figures are taken from lists published in the *Tuskegee News*.

The figures in Table III-1 show that the Negro proportion of the electorate continued to grow in spite of the ingenuity of white opponents. The important things to remember for the later analysis are that as early as 1952 Negroes constituted over a third of the electorate, that by 1960 they were virtually a half, and that beyond that date they were a substantial majority.

The story of the growth of Negro registration in Durham is rather less dramatic than Tuskegee's. Years have passed since systematic and widespread efforts were made to hinder Negroes from registering there, and indeed, white candidates seem to have played an important role in getting Negroes registered in the first place. Negro 'wardheelers' would tell candidates and factions that they would support them in the election if they would only see to it that Negroes were registered. Apparently numerous candidates complied with the suggestion. Surely one of the reasons that Durham whites felt they could afford to support registration of Negroes while Tuskegee went to such lengths to avoid it was that in the latter city Negroes were a potential majority, while in the former they were not. With time the system became one in which blocs of Negro votes were controlled by such wardheelers who would promise to deliver them for cash.[4] Disgust at this sort of activity was one of the stimuli for the establishment of the Durham Committee on Negro Affairs (DCNA) in 1935.

[3] This chronology is taken from Jones and Smith, *op. cit.*, ch. 2.
[4] See Harry J. Walker, "Changes in Race Accommodation in a Southern Community" (Unpublished Ph.D. dissertation, University of Chicago, 1945), pp. 197-204.

TABLE III-2

Negro Registration in Durham County[a]

Year	Total Negro Registration Number	Percentage of Eligible Negroes Registered	Percentage of Registered Negro Voters
1928	50	Not available	Not available
1935	1,000	" "	" "
1939	3,000	26.5%	13.1%
1958	12,209	60.7	23.7
1960	13,201	67.8	22.2

[a] The 1928 and 1935 figures come from interviews, and as with the 1939 figure, their roundness raises doubts about their accuracy, although they were reportedly based on actual counts. The 1939 figures come from Ralph J. Bunche, *The Political Status of the Negro* (1940); Microfilm, "Problems of the American Negro" in the New York Public Library, 135th St. Branch, Schomburg Collection, Film 326.998a, Reels 2 and 3, Accession Nos. 288, 289, Bk. II, chap. v, Reel 2, p. 568. The 1958 figures come from U. S., Commission on Civil Rights, *Report* (Washington: U. S. Government Printing Office, 1959), p. 570. The 1960 figures come from U. S. Commission on Civil Rights, *Report,* Vol. I, *Voting* (Washington: U. S. Government Printing Office, 1961), pp. 278-79.

Table III-2 shows that the number of Negroes registered in Durham County has gone up from a negligible fifty in 1928 to a very respectable 13,000 in 1960. Figures on percentage of voting age Negroes registered are not available before 1939, but go up from about one-fourth at that time to two-thirds in 1960. The significance of having 67.8 percent of the eligible Negro voters registered in 1960 becomes clearer when one notes that at the same time, only 38.2 percent of North Carolina's eligible Negroes were registered. In Virginia, only 46.2 percent of the *white* population was registered, and 23.0 percent of the Negroes. In Mississippi, only 6.2 percent of the Negroes were registered.

Such figures on the number and percentage of Negroes registered are the ones most often quoted to indicate the progress of the Negro in gaining the franchise. The percentage of the total registered electorate that is Negro is probably a more significant index of Negro voting strength, in that it reflects the significance of Negro votes relative to the voting population as a whole, and is a better reflection of the importance of Negro votes in determining electoral victory or defeat. This figure went up from a not insignificant 13.1 percent in 1939 to a very healthy 22-23 percent in the more recent period. Because 78.8 percent of Durham County Negroes live in the city of Durham, while only 65.7 percent of Durham County whites do, one may conclude that Negroes constitute an even higher proportion of city than county voters.

Some of the gaps in this information can be filled by figures reported in Table III-3 on the percentage of the *city* registered electorate constituted by the all Negro precincts. While they are in no sense accurate figures on percentage of the city electorate Negro, they are *minimum* figures and thus worth knowing.

TABLE III–3

Registration and Turnout in Durham Negro Precincts
as Percentage of Total City Registration and Turnout[a]

Year	Negro Precincts as Percent of City Registration	Negro Precincts as Percent of City Vote
1935	NA[b]	11.3%
1937	NA	13.4
1939	NA	11.7
1941	NA	14.8
1943	NA	13.0
1945	NA	16.2
1947	NA	16.5
1949	NA	16.6
1951	17.0%	17.1
1953	14.6	22.2
1955	14.7	19.3
1957	15.2	24.8
1959	NA	37.8
1961	NA	24.1
1963	25.3	26.4
1965	24.4	28.2
1967	21.0	22.0

[a] Figures in this and subsequent tables in this chapter are taken from official city election returns in city clerk's files, or if unavailable there, from returns in *Durham Morning Herald*.
[b] NA: not available

The fact that these precincts constituted in 1963 only 63 percent of Durham's Negro population emphasizes the fact that these figures are conservative. Negroes apparently constitute a formidable number of registered voters in Durham. The following pages will deal with the question of how effectively Negroes use this potential bloc.

TURNOUT OF NEGRO VOTERS[5]

Registration, of course, has no impact on the outcome of elections unless people vote. Because nonvoting is not randomly distributed throughout the population of eligible votes, some groups are likely to be disadvantaged by low turnout, even after they are registered.[6] Ne-

[5] Political subdivisions in Tuskegee do not yield data on the dimensions of voting strength taken up in the remainder of this chapter, which will as a consequence be devoted almost entirely to Durham.
[6] See Seymour Martin Lipset, *Political Man* (Garden City, New York: Doubleday and Co., Inc., 1959), ch. 6.

groes are usually among such groups. In many places where great efforts have been expended to register Negroes, discouragingly high numbers fail to turn out.

This has not been a problem in Durham. Table III-3 shows that the Negro precincts have made up a sizeable proportion of Durham's voting electorate since 1935. More importantly, whenever available data allow a comparison of the proportion of total registration to proportion of total turnout in these precincts, these Negroes are *more* rather than less likely to turn out to vote than other registrants! Turnout is actually higher in the Negro than in the other precincts.

Thus, while even in Durham mobilizing Negroes for political purposes by registering them to vote is harder, the payoff or efficiency from those registered is greater than usual there, because registered Negroes there are even more likely to turn out than white voters—at least in city elections. The higher turnout in Negro precincts can without much doubt be attributed to the superior political organization of the Negro community, and to the efforts of the DCNA to get voters to the polls on election day.

COHESION OF NEGRO VOTERS

In democratic politics candidates commonly make appeals to various important groups of voters and the voters respond to the more effective appeals with support at the polls. Often the signals by which candidates show where they stand are quite subtle. For example, Barry Goldwater's campaign speeches on violence in the streets were interpreted by white and Negro alike as an anti-civil rights appeal.[7] On sensitive issues like race, candidates are often considerably more subtle than Goldwater if they give any signals at all. Consequently the Negro voter may have difficulty identifying his friends, or may respond to candidates in the same way that whites with very different preferences on racial issues do.[8] The Negro voter may need help in identifying which candidates are likely to do the most for him. In Durham and Tuskegee, such cues are provided by Negro political organizations which recommend or endorse candidates.

The political arm of the Tuskegee Civic Association, the Macon

---

[7] But see James Q. Wilson, "The Negro in Politics," in Talcott Parsons and Kenneth B. Clark, eds., *The Negro American* (Boston: The Beacon Press, 1967), pp. 436-37.
[8] For example, in Raleigh, North Carolina's 1963 city council election there was a rank order correlation of .84 between the vote in five virtually all Negro precincts containing 86 percent of the city's registered Negroes and the vote in the other thirty precincts.

County Democratic Club (MCDC) is the agency that provides recommendations in Tuskegee elections. The decision to recommend a candidate is made by a vote of the membership at meetings held the Monday night before each election, but the organization has a very laissez-faire style of implementing this decision. The MCDC's leaders emphasize that members remain free to vote for whom they please and that no armtwisting is involved. Even the car pools are voluntary and not official. The voter assumes responsibility for getting himself to the polls, though he may request help.

The Durham Committee on Negro Affairs (DCNA) has quite a different approach. Candidates for public office are invited to appear before the membership and appeal for support some time before the election. Subsequently the Political Committee of the organization meets and decides on its recommendations for endorsement, which it places before the membership on the night before an election. After discussion of the recommendations, they are subjected to a vote which constitutes endorsement. The style is considerably less laissez-faire than that of the MCDC. The DCNA's leaders articulately defend the recommendations that they have agreed upon before, using their considerable powers of persuasion and the powers of the platform to assure that they are rarely voted down. Endorsements are printed up overnight and distributed to Negroes at the polls throughout election day. The emphasis is not on every man being free to accept or ignore the recommendations, but rather on the importance of cohesion to insure that the endorsed candidates receive a maximum of votes from the Negro community. Also, the organization takes considerably more initiative than the MCDC in seeing to it that a maximum of Negro voters get to the polls.

Unlike those in Tuskegee, Durham's voting records allow a measure of the success of its Negro organization in mobilizing a vote for its endorsees. This will be done by investigating the division of the votes in the all Negro precincts. While these precincts contain virtually no whites, they do not contain all of the Negroes in the city. There are several other smaller Negro residential areas in the city which are also represented by the DCNA. Voters in the all-Negro precincts, which contain by far the largest concentration of Negroes in the city, are probably somewhat more cohesive than those elsewhere, simply because it is easier to mobilize voters that are so concentrated. Still, the figures cited above on turnout in these precincts make it clear that a highly cohesive vote in these precincts alone is an important bloc even if other Negroes were to vote randomly.

While the cohesion of the Negro vote was erratic and never over 86 percent in the period from 1937-1947 (see Table III-4), it has been remarkable in the period since then. In the earlier period, the average vote in Negro precincts for the leading candidate there in contested two-man elections was 72.9 percent, while from 1949-1967 it was 91.0. The all Negro precincts gave 85 percent or more of their vote to the DCNA endorsee in twenty-six of the twenty-eight contested two-man elections in the later period.

TABLE III–4

Voting Cohesion in Contested Two-Man Elections in Durham's Negro Precincts, 1937-1967[a]

Percentage for Leading Candidate	Number of Elections		
	1937-1947	*1949-1967*	*Total*
95-100	..	9	9
90-94.9	..	8	8
85-89.9	2	9	11
80-84.9	5	0	5
75-79.9	5	0	5
70-74.9	7	1	8
65-69.9	3	1	4
60-64.9	2	..	2
55-69.9	2	..	2
50-54.9	2	..	2
Total	28	28	56

[a] All figures for the period 1949-1967 are for the DCNA endorsee. Figures for the period 1937-1947 are simply for the leading candidate in the Negro precincts, because the endorsee is not known in all cases.

The number of elections in which 85 percent or more of the vote was delivered to the endorsee is indeed remarkable, but how must we interpret the two elections in which the endorsee received less than that figure? The two occasions in which the all Negro precincts delivered less than 85 percent of their vote to the endorsee are easy to explain, although they do define certain limits on DCNA influence over the Negro voters. In 1957, J. S. Stewart carried these precincts by only 74.2 percent of the vote cast. What was unusual about the election was that both Stewart and his opponent were Negroes. Both men were well known and respected in the Negro community. Stewart was an official of the Negro owned savings and loan association; and Taylor, his opponent, was a Dean at North Carolina College, the state college for Negroes in Durham, and one of the founders of the DCNA. Under such circumstances, Stewart's total may be considered high, rather than low.

In 1961, J. Leslie Atkins, Jr., received only 68.7 percent of the vote for mayor coming from the Negro precincts. What made this election unusual was that Atkins' opponent was Mayor E. J. Evans, whom the DCNA had endorsed previously each time he had faced opposition. Evans had been mayor for ten years and had built up something of a reputation as a liberal and a friend of the Negro community. Atkins, on the other hand, had been the engineer of a Negro-liberal-labor coalition that had gained control of the county Democratic party and had been influential in local politics for about ten years.

One of the most explicit tests of DCNA influence over Negro voters took place in the 1965 primary. David Stith, Negro president of a local business college, challenged incumbent Negro councilman J. S. Stewart, who is a highly influential member of the DCNA. While Stith sought (and lost) DCNA endorsement, he campaigned on the theme that the current Negro councilman had been letting down the Negro community, and he let it be known that he was dissatisfied with the current leadership of the DCNA. In a three-man primary race involving these two men and a white candidate, Stewart polled 70.9 percent of the vote in the Negro precincts to Stith's 28.1 percent. In the 1953 Ward Three primary, the only other occasion when Negro ran against Negro, the endorsee received only 61 percent of the votes in Negro precincts. This was more a split of personalities than an explicit challenge to the organization.

The picture is similar in the races for the three at-large seats, although the DCNA seems slightly less potent here. As described in chapter II, each elector can vote for three candidates in a field of as many as six in these at-large races. On occasion, however, the bullet or single-shot vote is used to maximize the chances of a given candidate for victory. This involves voting for only one candidate, in many cases a Negro, so as not to help any of his opponents. Using the other votes for other candidates may give them the margin of victory over the candidate most preferred by the DCNA.

There have been eleven of these at-large elections in Durham since they were first instituted in 1947. In six of these, the DCNA endorsed the maximum of three candidates; and in each of these six, the three candidates together received over 89 percent of the vote in the Negro precincts. The DCNA has been somewhat less efficient in single- or double-shot voting, which they tried in the first two and the last three elections of the series. In 1947, the two white candidates they endorsed received 76.0 percent of the Negro precincts' vote. I have already pointed out that the DCNA was less effective overall before 1949. In the following election, in 1949, the DCNA bullet-endorsed a white candidate, who received only 59 percent of the Negro precincts' vote. The next six elections involved successful triple endorsements (over 89 percent cohesion). In 1963, 1965 and 1967 the DCNA has given a single-shot endorsement to Negro candidates, for whom it was able to deliver 83.7, 81.4 and 86.4 percent of the vote in Negro precincts, respectively.

This should not be interpreted as meaning that the DCNA is less effective in endorsing Negroes than whites. The nature of bullet voting itself is a much more plausible explanation. The reduced efficiency of the DCNA's endorsements in elections where it recommends a bullet vote is probably in large part the result of confusion on the part of the voters. Their sample ballot from the DCNA tells them to vote for one candidate and the voting machine tells them to vote for three. Under such circumstances it may be as much an indication of strength as of weakness that the organization can deliver so much of the Negro vote to a single candidate in a race for three seats.

Bond issue elections are another reflection of the efficiency with which the Negro vote is organized. For this reason, and also because they will be shown to be an important source of Negro political influence, I will briefly treat Negro voting in such elections.

The DCNA endorsed fifty-six of the sixty-one questions in the fifteen bond issue and special tax elections held since 1945, delivering an average of 91.0 percent of the vote in the Negro precincts to whichever side, pro or con, it had endorsed. Table III-5 shows that cohesion

TABLE III–5

The Negro Vote in Durham Bond Issue and Special Tax Elections
(1947-1966)

Year	Number of Questions	Number Endorsed by DCNA	Cohesion of Negro Precincts	Questions with DCNA on Winning Side	Questions Controlled by DCNA[a]
1947	10	10	93.2%	90%	10%
1948	1	1	94.5	100	0
1950	2	2	94.1	100	0
1951	10	9	77.8	70	60
1952	1	1	92.0	100	0
1954	2	2	94.3	100	100
1956	8	8	93.0	100	100
1958	1	1	96.8	100	100
1958	1	0	88.8	100	0
1959	8	8	95.2	100	87.5
1960	1	0	87.5	0	0
1962	8	8	92.1	100	100
1964	1	0	84.2	0	0
1965	6	6	93.5	100	0
1966	1	0	88.2	100	0
Total	61	56	..	..	..
Average	..	..	91.0%	90.2%	54.1%

[a] Questions whose outcome would have been different if the vote in the Negro precincts had been reversed.

33

was lowest in the five elections in which the DCNA did not endorse a question. In fact, these are the only five elections in which cohesion was below 90 percent. There were four elections in which the DCNA advised its members to vote "no," in which the rates of cohesion were 89, 88, 84 and 88 percents. In another, the DCNA endorsed nine out of ten questions, and cohesion dropped to 78 percent. This appears to be at least partly because of confusion, because electors were instructed to vote "yes" on the first seven, "no" on number eight and "yes" on nine and ten.

DELIVERABILITY

Hugh Douglas Price, Harry Holloway and Allan Sindler have each pointed out that a cohesive Negro bloc vote is not necessarily an independent, manipulable political force.[9] They suggest that parties and voters' leagues get credit for sending the Negro vote in the same direction that it would have gone anyway, and that the Negro vote is usually not deliverable. What evidence is there that the high degree of support for DCNA endorsees in Negro precincts is not simply a situation in which the organization happens to endorse the candidates the Negro voters would have chosen anyway?

If we know nothing else, we might reasonably infer deliverability from the fact that the elections in question are nonpartisan, and that there are no party cues for the voters. We might surmise that most voters do not have the kind of information that would allow for such cohesive voting without organizational guidance. Indeed, that Durham Negroes vote as they do because of independent evaluations is surely a less plausible hypothesis than that they do so because of the endorsement of the DCNA.

Fortunately we are not dependent on such inferences. There are some empirical data which make the impact of the DCNA endorsement clearer and more remarkable. There have been several instances in which the organization has withdrawn its support from someone who previously had had it, or has endorsed someone who had previously failed to get the nod.

Table III-6 shows the vote in Negro precincts for all candidates for city council from 1945 to 1967 who were endorsed in at least one

[9] Hugh Douglas Price, *The Negro and Southern Politics* (New York: New York University Press, 1957), p. 74. Harry Holloway, "The Negro and the Vote: The Case of Texas," *Journal of Politics*, XXIII (1961), pp. 539-40. Allan P. Sindler, "Protest Against the Political Status of the Negro," *The Annals of the American Academy of Political and Social Science*, CCCLVII, p. 52.

TABLE III–6
Changes in DCNA Endorsement and the Vote for City
Council in Negro Precincts

Name of Candidate	Year	Office	Percentage of Vote in Negro Precincts	Endorsed
Gregory[1]	1947	Ward 4	75.0%	Yes
	1951	Ward 4	13.9	No
Evans[1]	1951	Mayor	95.7	Yes
	1957	Mayor	92.9	Yes
	1961	Mayor	31.5	No
Moss[1]	1945	Ward 4	70.8	Yes
	1949	A.L.	6.9	No
Mumford[1]	1945	Ward 2	64.8	Yes
	1949	A.L.	5.3	No
Whitfield[1]	1951	A.L.	1.4	No
	1953	Ward 5	89.6	Yes
Dean[1]	1961	Ward 5	88.9	Yes
	1965	Ward 5	3.7	No
Williamson[2]	1949	A.L.	59.0	Yes[B]
	1953	A.L.	31.0	Yes
	1963	A.L.	4.4	No
Biggs[2]	1947	A.L.	7.8	No
	1955	A.L.	31.2	Yes
	1957	Mayor	7.1	No
	1959	A.L.	31.7	Yes
	1967	Ward 4	6.6	No
Barbour[2]	1955	A.L.	30.9	Yes
	1959	A.L.	31.6	Yes
	1963	A.L.	4.1	No
	1967	A.L.	5.9	No
Strawbridge[2]	1947	A.L.	6.3	No
	1951	A.L.	17.2	Yes[a]
	1953	A.L.	30.9	Yes
Taylor[2] (Negro)	1951	A.L.	50.9	Yes
	1953	Ward 3	39.2	No[b]
	1957	Ward 3	25.8	No
Alford[2]	1961	A.L.	31.7	Yes
	1965	A.L.	5.5	No
Carleton[2]	1961	A.L.	31.4	Yes
	1965	A.L.	4.2	No
Steel[2]	1961	A.L.	28.9	Yes
	1965	A.L.	5.7	No
Grabarek[3]	1957	A.L.	31.4	Yes
	1963	Mayor	89.2	Yes
	1965	Mayor	97.9	Yes
	1967	Mayor	11.3	No

Legend: 1 = candidates endorsed in a two-man race; 2 = candidates endorsed in an at-large race; 3 = candidate endorsed in both; A.L. = at-large; B = bullet.
[a] In race with Taylor, a Negro.
[b] Three-man primary.

race and not in another. In the ward and mayoralty races, perfect efficiency of endorsement would involve 100 percent for the endorsed candidate and 0 percent of the vote for the unendorsed. In at-large contests 33.3 percent of the vote for endorsees and 0 percent for the unendorsed is perfect efficiency. The one exception to this rule is the case of Williamson, endorsed in an at-large race, for whom 100 percent would have been perfect, because he was the subject of a bullet endorsement. Note also that Taylor received 17.6 percent more than perfect efficiency would have given him; apparently a good number of Negroes bullet voted for him because he was a Negro, even though he did not receive bullet endorsement.

Taylor, being a Negro, was one candidate for whom endorsements were quite inefficient. As noted above, he got more than DCNA endorsement was prepared to give him in 1951, and in 1953 he got almost 40 percent of the Negro vote even though unendorsed. Ignoring him, the deliverability of the Negro vote is remarkably efficient. Candidates who were unendorsed in at least one race, and endorsed in a two-man race (denoted by a 1) all experienced a gain or loss of at least 60 percentage points of the vote in the Negro precincts, except one who lost only 59.6 points. This was in the period before peak efficiency had been reached. Two lost or gained over 85 points.

All candidates who were endorsed in an at-large race and not endorsed in another (denoted by a 2), for whom a 33.3 percentage point change would have been perfect efficiency, experienced at least a 23 point change, except for the time when Strawbridge was endorsed with Taylor; and four of the seven experienced a change of over 25 points. The experience of Biggs is especially suggestive. He went from 8 to 31, back to 7, up to 32 and back to 7 percent again with the gain or loss of endorsement. When endorsed, he received almost perfect support.[10]

BALANCE OF POWER

If Negro votes, or any other votes, are important, we expect them to have some effect on the behavior of candidates. We expect candidates and potential candidates to take the preferences of voters into account when they decide whether or not to run, and when they take their stands on public issues. It seems reasonable to expect that these votes will have the greatest impact on the behavior of candidates when they are the most crucial to victory. A candidate who would win even if

---

[10] The discussion of cohesion in bond issue elections, *supra* pp. 33-34, is the equivalent of a discussion of deliverability in bond elections. See Table III-5.

all the Negro votes were against him would not be expected to be as sensitive to Negro demands and interests as a candidate who would have lost without Negro votes. Because of this, several questions should be raised about the importance of Negro votes to the victory of city council candidates and bond issue questions in Durham in the period from 1937 to 1967.

As in the section on cohesion, I will separate the data on candidates into two groups, this time from 1937 through 1945 and from 1947 through 1965. There are three reasons for this breakdown. First and most important, the year 1946 divides a period in which votes in Negro precincts meant very little in determining the outcome of elections from one in which they appear to be rather important. Secondly, not all of the endorsees are known for the earlier period. Thirdly, and only coincidentally, 1947 marks the first year that the ward and at-large election system described in chapter II was instituted. Before that time, all councilmen were elected the way the present ward candidates are elected.

First, I will measure the number of times candidates were unopposed. Lack of opposition may be an indication that other candidates have not run because they felt it would be hopeless without Negro support. It may, on the other hand, be merely an indication of a lack of interest in running for office, or of general satisfaction with current candidates and incumbents. In the absence of any concrete information, none of these assumptions should be made. The question should be left open.

In two types of elections for mayor or a ward seat, I will conclude that the importance of the Negro vote for the outcome is low, and assume that the Negroes did not provide a balance of power: those in which the leading candidate in the Negro precincts lost, and those in which the winner's margin of victory was so great that Negro votes could not have changed the outcome. I will isolate the latter category by identifying those candidates who would have won even if the Negro precincts' vote for the two candidates had been reversed. I will assume, on the basis of the section above on deliverability of the vote, that the DCNA could have delivered to the unendorsed candidate the same proportion of Negro votes that it delivered to the endorsee. While this probably overestimates DCNA influence in many cases, particularly before 1949, it is compensated for by the fact that there are other Negro votes in other Negro precincts that would probably have been reversed. If such a reversal would not have cost the leading candidate the election, I will conclude that the Negroes did not hold a balance of power and that they did not control the outcome of the election.

In two types of elections, I will consider that DCNA influence is high and indeed a balance of power. This category includes candidates who would have lost if the Negro precincts were excluded from the totals, or for whom a reversal of the votes in the Negro precincts as outlined above would have changed the outcome of the election.

According to the figures in Table III-7, Negro votes were decisive in none of the contests for mayor before 1946, and in only one-fifth of the contested elections for ward seats in that period. They were decisive in only 13.3 percent of all ward contests before 1946. The picture is quite different in the period since then. Negro votes were important in determining the outcome of 57 percent of the contested elections for mayor and in 36 percent of all the later mayoralty elections. Similarly, Negro votes were decisive in 61 percent of the contested ward elections after 1946, and in 42 percent of all ward contests in that period.

TABLE III-7

Influence of the Negro Vote on the Outcome of Durham Ward and Mayoralty Elections, 1937-1965

	1937-1945		1947-1965	
Item	*for mayor*	*for ward seats*	*for mayor*	*for ward seats*
I. Candidate unopposed.	2	7	4	10
II. Negro influence low.				
A. Candidate leading in Negro precincts lost.	1	3	2	5
B. Margin of victory too great to be affected by reversal of votes in Negro precincts.	2	16	1	4
III. Negro influence high.				
A. Candidate leading in Negro precincts would have lost if Negro precincts were excluded from totals.	0	2	3	8
B. Candidate leading in Negro precincts would have lost if vote in Negro precincts had been reversed.	0	2	1	6
Total	5	30	11	33

For the at-large seats, the situation is less clear, and seemingly less favorable to Negro influence. Only four of the 33 seats (all since 1946) would have changed hands if the Negro precincts had been omitted from the election totals. However, if we take into account the power of the DCNA to manipulate the vote, it might have affected the outcome of the contest for 13 of the 33 seats by various combinations of endorsements.

Overall, the Negro vote was actually or potentially controlling in 31 of 63 contested elections between 1947 and 1967, or almost half. It was important in two-fifths of all 77 elections in that period.

How was this influence distributed over time in the two periods? How close do the Negroes come to influencing the election of a majority of the members of a given council? Table III-8 shows that the low influence in the early period and the high influence in the later one was

TABLE III–8

Number of Seats Actually or Potentially Under the
Control of the Vote in Durham's Negro Precincts

Council Term Beginning	Influenced Number (of 13)	Council Term Beginning	Influenced Number (of 13)
1937	0	1953	6
1939	2	1955	7
1941	2	1957	4
1943	2	1959	2
1945	2	1961	4
1947	5	1963	7
1949	8	1965	5
1951	4	1967	4

spread rather evenly in each of the respective times. No more than two seats were potentially controlled by the vote in the Negro precincts before 1947, and only once since then has the number fallen below four.

I do not mean to imply that this information reflects a precise measure of Negro influence over these councilmen. Indeed, there is little doubt that many of these people felt no special obligation to the Negro community at all. Also, their opponents may have preferred defeat to any change in behavior that would have made them more acceptable to the Negro voters. I will suggest later, however, that having an influence over the outcome of bond issue elections may be a more significant resource for influencing policy than influence over the outcome of candidate elections. Table III-5 (p. 33) shows that reversal of the vote in Negro precincts would have reversed the outcome of slightly over half of the bond issue questions put before Durham voters since 1945.

The major purpose of this chapter has been to describe changes in the level of Negro voting strength in Tuskegee and Durham, in anticipation of relating them to changes in policy outputs to Negroes. The important change in Tuskegee was that from a minority to a majority of the electorate. In Durham the point that I will return to most often is that Negroes there had developed a sizeable, cohesive and deliverable vote by the end of the 1940's.

CHAPTER IV

The Payoffs of Negro Voting: The Public Sector

Now THAT WE have assessed Negro voting strength in the two cities, we are ready to evaluate its impact. We are ready to see whether, with the right to vote assured, "all other rights are potentially assured," and whether the vote is in fact "the most powerful instrument ever devised by man for breaking down injustice."[1] In what ways has life improved for Negroes in Durham and Tuskegee as a result of voting? Are Negroes really noticeably better off because they exercise the right to vote?

Two basic considerations will guide this investigation. One is the body of knowledge the book addresses, and the other is the nature of political goals sought after by Negroes. This is a book on political science, and one of the basic concerns of that discipline is public policy. We think votes are important in a democracy because they help determine who takes office, and by extension what public policies elected officials will formulate. Consequently the book will focus on how effectively Negro votes implement Negro goals by seeing to what extent the votes secure public policies which bring them about. Public policy will be construed broadly to include all official actions by government, or, following Easton, all "authoritative allocations of value"[2] on matters of interest to Negroes. Consequently I will not look for every increase in the enjoyment of life's advantages by Negroes, but only at those which are brought about (by voting) through some sort of governmental action.

The second consideration which focuses this inquiry involves what

[1] See above, pp. 1-2.
[2] See David Easton, *The Political System* (New York: Alfred A. Knopf, 1953), ch. 5.

I will view as being of interest to Negroes. Studying policy outputs of relevance to Negroes is different from studying those of interest to other population groupings such as doctors, farmers, businessmen or veterans. Interest groups may be defined by any shared characteristic which is relevant to their political behavior.[3] The crucial "shared characteristic" of Negroes, their race, does not have anything directly to do with such attributes as occupational goals or the abstract political values which motivate much interest group activity. The reason the Negro's race is so important is that it has been a mark of discrimination and subordination ever since Negroes have been on the American continent.

The subject of this and the next chapter, then, is public policy outputs which eliminate or mitigate discrimination and the effects of discrimination against Negroes. The point is not to look for policies that do special favors for Negroes, as tariffs, depletion allowances and low cost postal rates do for businessmen, or veterans' benefits do for veterans. The policy outputs toward Negroes with which the book is primarily concerned are not favors but more accurately the rights of equal treatment and full participation in the benefits of society. Negroes have been segregated and mistreated in both the public or governmental sector of social life and also in the private sector for hundreds of years. This chapter is devoted to the role of the vote in eliminating discrimination at the hands of government itself. The next will deal with the impact of the vote on public policies which are designed to eliminate private discrimination and the effects of past discrimination.[4]

[3] See David B. Truman, *The Governmental Process* (New York: Alfred A. Knopf, 1951), ch. 2.

[4] For other literature on the effects of Negro voting, see: Ralph T. Bunche, *The Political Status of the Negro* (1940), Microfilm, "Problems of the American Negro" in New York Public Library, 135th St. Branch, Schomburg Collection, Film 326. M998a, Reels 2 & 3, Accession Nos. 288 and 289, Book VI, ch. 18, Reel 3, pp. 1472-475; Alfred B. Clubok, John M. DeGrove and Charles D. Farris, "The Manipulated Negro Vote: Some Pre-Conditions and Consequences," *Journal of Politics,* XXVI (1964), pp. 112-29; Harold F. Gosnell, *Negro Politicians* (Chicago: University of Chicago Press, 1935), p. 370; Harry Holloway, "The Negro and the Vote: The Case of Texas," *Journal of Politics,* XXIII (1961), pp. 525-56; V. O. Key, Jr., *Southern Politics* (New York: Alfred A. Knopf, 1949), p. 508; Key, *Politics, Parties and Pressure Groups* (5th ed.; New York: Thomas Y. Crowell Co., 1964), p. 623; Robert E. Lane, *Political Life* (Glencoe, Ill.: The Free Press, 1959), p. 338; Gunnar Myrdal, *An American Dilemma* (New York: McGraw-Hill Book Co., 1964), pp. 497-504; Allan Sindler, "Protest against the Political Status of the Negro," *Annals of the American Academy of Political and Social Science,* CCCLVII (1965), pp. 48-54; John H. Strange, "The Negro in Philadelphia Politics: 1963-1965 " (Unpublished Ph.D. Dissertation, Princeton University, 1966); Stephen Whitaker, "A New Day: The Effects of Negro Enfranchisement in Selected Mississippi Counties " (Unpublished Ph.D. dissertation, Florida State University, 1965); and U. S., Commission on Civil Rights, *Report,* Vol. I, *Voting* (Washington: U. S. Government Printing Office, 1961), Part III.

THE OUTCOME OF ELECTIONS

To turn directly to policy outputs that can be traced to Negro voting would be premature, because this would ignore the process through which outputs are influenced. The most obvious and direct result of voting is the outcome of elections, and presumably whatever influence Negroes have on policy is a result of their ability to influence such outcomes. We have seen in the preceding chapter that in Durham at least, Negro influence over the outcome of elections is quite high, but that chapter did not point out how often the preferred alternatives of each Negro organization prevailed. This section will report how often the endorsees of the DCNA and the MCDC won elections, and how often Negro candidates were elected to office, as an intervening variable between votes and policy.

SUCCESS OF ENDORSEES. Tuskegee's MCDC has been "recommending" support of various candidates since about 1954, but has not so endorsed candidates in all races. Their rate of success is remarkably high, and as we will see a far cry beyond their success rate in policy outputs for most of the period studied. According to MCDC leaders, no candidate for whom support was recommended in the final election ever failed to win, although several candidates endorsed in primaries were not elected.

When we see how restricted the policy payoffs were in Tuskegee for most of this period, we cannot take such a success record too seriously. As an index of success in politics, it can be inflated in two ways: either by recommending the probable winner and predicting well, or by making recommendations in so few elections as to give the recommendations more meaning, but narrower coverage. There appear to be elements of both factors in Tuskegee. MCDC success in securing policy goals before 1964 makes it apparent that they either endorsed some candidates who offered very little to the Negro community or never endorsed enough to have much of an impact on policy.

The limitations on choice that can be imposed by available candidates are well illustrated by the experience of Negroes who constituted a fifth of the registered electorate in a rural Virginia county I visited. A number of people in the county were asked what the effects of Negro voting had been, and what, if anything, Negroes had gained from their enfranchisement. There was only one incident that anyone, white or Negro, could recall that came close to reflecting Negro influence. Political conflicts in the county's dominant Democratic party were based on personality differences within that unanimity about important social issues that pervades white political attitudes in such heavily Negro rural southern locales. There was no recognized attempt to appeal for the Negro vote by making any sorts of promises, even though the competition was occasionally stiff. This amounted to a tacit agreement by white candidates, dictated by the mores of the county and by the certain fate of anyone who did appeal actively for Negro votes.

On only one occasion were there differences between candidates that were in any way pertinent to the interests of the Negro. On this occasion, one candidate for office was known to have made a George Wallace-like statement about what he would do if any "Nigger" tried to enter the county's white high school. Because this statement became known, this candidate became the anti-Negro candidate. The Negroes voted against him, and informed persons of both races agreed that a Negro balance of power had defeated him.

This is an example of an extremely rudimentary form of Negro voting power. Negro votes were said to have determined the outcome, but their alternatives were such as to be almost useless to them in all but a symbolic sense. No white or Negro interviewed could think of any way in which the candidate the Negroes voted for and put into office was more favorable to their interests than the one they defeated. The one candidate was apparently as good and reliable a segregationist as the other. There was no reason to believe that public policy in that county would be any different under the one man as opposed to the other.

This incident reveals one possible effect of Negro voting on the outcome of elections: the defeat of race-baiting candidates. The concrete advantages resulting from this are nil. To select the milder sounding of alternatives that behaviorally mean the same thing is only a symbolic gain. Nevertheless, this is progress. Such incidents will probably contribute to the development of a sense of political efficacy among Negroes, and lift the morale of their political leaders. It may also contribute to a long term trend among white candidates to come closer and closer to appealing for Negro votes.

In Durham, every one of the post-war candidates for city council which the DCNA endorsed in advance of the primary entered the general election. Seventy-five percent of the candidates endorsed for the general election won seats on the council. Since being a Negro is a disadvantage for a candidate in Durham, as elsewhere in the South where candidates are elected at large in communities with white majorities, this success rate is all the more remarkable when one considers that six of the fourteen defeated endorsees were Negro, and that five of the forty-three successful ones were Negro.

The overall rate of success disguises an important change that reflects a change in DCNA strategy. From 1945 to 1953, only 62.5 percent of the endorsees were successful, but since then, 84.8 percent of those selected have won office.[5] The five failures in the later period include two Negroes running at large and two opponents to incumbent mayors. At what cost did the DCNA increase its "success"? Possibly, the price was endorsing candidates who were less sympathetic to Negro interests, but who at the same time had a better chance of winning.

Documentation for this viewpoint appears in an article by Lewis Bowman and Robert Boynton on the Durham situation.[6] The authors describe Voters for Better Government (VBG), a coalition of the DCNA, labor, and liberal academic and business factions in Durham, lasting from about 1947 to 1958. Although this coalition was not the same thing as the DCNA, the two were closely allied during the life of the VBG.

Bowman and Boynton divide the candidates supported by the coalition into members (30.5 percent), persons on the fringe of the coalition (30.5 percent) and independents endorsed by the coalition (39 percent). I will consider these concepts an index of the closeness of the relationship between the DCNA and these candidates. The authors show how the distribution of endorsees among the three groups changed somewhat over the period before and after the 1954 school desegregation decision. While the percentage of endorsees from the fringe of the coalition remained just under 40 percent in both the 1949-1953 and 1953-1957 periods, 50 percent of the endorsees were *members* of the coalition before the Brown decision and only 8 percent afterwards. Similarly, only 11 percent of the endorsees were independents before the decision but 54 percent afterwards.[7]

The point to be made is that the intensification of the race issue after the Supreme Court made it more salient in 1954 put the Voters for Better Government on the defensive, and caused it to nominate fewer of its own candidates. As shown by rank order correlation, the sources of support for the coalition's candidates changed somewhat over the period before and after 1954, but while one would anticipate that the

[5] There were twenty-four endorsees in the earlier period and thirty-three endorsees in the later period. Although there are seven winners in every election, the numbers are not multiples of seven because of 'bullet' or 'single-shot' votes in elections for the three large seats. If the DCNA was especially interested in electing one at–large candidate, usually a Negro, it would endorse only one of the candidates even though each voter could vote for three of the six men running. This way they would not give any votes to a less preferred candidate, who might push the chosen one out of the top three.

[6] "Coalition as Party in a One-Party Southern Area: A Theoretical and Case Analysis," *Midwest Journal of Political Science*, VIII (1964), pp. 277-97.

[7] *Ibid.*, p. 288.

coalition would have been disadvantaged by the Brown decision, the reverse was the case, on the surface at least.[8]

Before 1954, only eleven of the coalition's eighteen candidates won. After that date, all thirteen endorsees won. The change in endorsement policy may be used to explain the increased success after the school decision. Of the seven candidates which were defeated (all, it will be remembered, before 1954) six were members of the coalition, and one was a fringe candidate. Thus by making their modal candidate the independent rather than the member, "they insured their success at the polls by sacrificing the former closeness of the relationship between the candidate and the coalition."[9]

This increased success of coalition candidates is congruent with the increase in the success of DCNA endorsees described above. Presumably this increased success also involved a sacrifice of closeness of the relationship between the candidate and the DCNA. The above account of the coalition serves the purpose of providing evidence to that effect for the period from 1949 to 1957, and it also illustrates the point about tactics of influence.

The payoffs of winning bond issue elections are somewhat more concrete than those of successfully placing endorsees in office, and, as I will argue later in this chapter, bond elections are a somewhat more useful channel of Negro voting influence than are candidate elections for many purposes. Table III-5 (p. 33) shows that the DCNA was quite successful in bond elections, being on the winning side in 90.2 percent of the contests since the war. However useful bond issue elections have been in Durham, they have been no help to Tuskegee Negroes, because Tuskegee has not used bond elections for city services as Durham has.

There are dilemmas of strategy for Negro political organizations representing a minority of the voters trying to secure concessions from a white majority which may be split on other issues. Alternatives are often almost equally unacceptable. The organization may choose to reward the slightest preferability with support, or it may use votes to punish officials who have not done enough, even if their opponents offer no more. The DCNA has followed the first strategy, and the MCDC the second.

The DCNA strategy as a rule has been to endorse the candidate who is most desirable or least undesirable in every election, no matter how miniscule the differences. This approach has two important consequences. It makes the endorsement relatively easy to get without

[8] *Ibid.,* p. 293.
[9] *Ibid.,* p. 295.

running risks of alienating white voters. White candidates do not have to bend over backwards outdoing their opponents in making themselves attractive to the DCNA. This makes life easier for the candidates, because the more they please the Negroes, the more risks they run with white voters. At the same time this strategy seems to avoid making the endorsement a 'kiss of death.' Being endorsed by the DCNA does not necessarily mean that a candidate is a radical liberal on the race issue even by Durham white standards. Endorsement means little enough about a candidate to be a rather innocuous factor. While it is not a positive advantage among white voters, it is not a very sharp disadvantage. In spite of the efforts of the DCNA to keep their endorsements secret before election day, they often become an open secret, even getting into the morning paper on election day, but this has not hurt the success rate appreciably. Some non-endorsees try to make the bloc vote an election issue, but while this may help them, it does not necessarily bring victory. Such persons are not much more likely to win if they are advantaged at all.

Tuskegee Negroes have a different approach. First, they do not necessarily make recommendations for every contest, as the DCNA does. Second, at least one of the MCDC's leaders articulated a strategy of opposing the incumbent whenever two undesirable candidates were running. The effect of this is to add to the incentives for candidates to 'earn' Negro support. If being one very small degree better than one's opponent from the Negro point of view is not enough to bring MCDC endorsement, there is reason to try to become 'enough better' to secure the endorsement. Similarly, voting against an incumbent when he has not cooperated has the advantage of 'punishing' him for his failure to cooperate rather than 'rewarding' him for not being any worse than his opponent. Again, it adds to the incentives to do something for the Negroes. This is to say that the endorsement of the MCDC with this strategy means more than that of the DCNA with its willingness to reward the most miniscule differences. In effect, the DCNA strategy responds to existing alternatives, while the MCDC tries to improve them.

However, at the same time that the endorsement means more, the other side of the coin is that it is more likely to cause a reaction among white voters—to be a kiss of death. The success rate of the MCDC in electing its endorsees makes it clear that this was not the problem in Tuskegee. The recommendation of the MCDC was anything but a kiss of death. The problem was rather that, whatever the merits of the strategy in abstract, the city council did virtually nothing for Tuskegee Negroes in the years before they were a majority. The strategy is appealing, and it might have done more for Durham Negroes than DCNA strategy did (I am inclined to think it would have) but resistance in Tuskegee was so high that it did the MCDC no good until as a majority they could pick and elect their own candidates.

ELECTION OF NEGROES. The number of Negro candidates elected to public office in Durham has always been very limited. Negroes have been running for city council there since 1945, but while one candidate received 45 percent of the total city vote in 1949, the first was not elected until 1953. There has been at least one Negro on the council ever since. Since 1963, Negro candidates have been trying regularly to take a second seat on the city council by running in at-large races, supported by single-shot or bullet endorsement of the DCNA.[10] One was finally successful in 1967, and there are currently two Negroes on a council of thirteen. Durham Negroes have not been successful in electing candidates for any county offices or for the state legislature, although Negroes have run for both. Each of the Negro precincts has elected Negro precinct chairmen and there has been a Negro justice of the peace for years.

So long as Tuskegee Negroes were a voting minority they had considerably less success, electing no Negroes to any public office even though they have constituted over a third of the electorate since 1952. The first Negro candidate was a woman who ran for county school board in 1954, the year of the Brown school desegregation decision. The tide turned sharply in 1964, however, after Negroes became a majority of the electorate. Since then, Negroes have been elected to two out of six of the seats on the city council, to two of five seats on the county board of revenue, to two of five seats on the board of education, to tax collector and, perhaps most remarkably, to sheriff. Six of the county's ten precinct chairmen and two of the three justices of the peace are now Negro.

Why a majority of the electorate has not put Negroes into all elected offices, as it did for whites, is pertinent to ask, as some Tuskegee Negroes have. The Negro community of Tuskegee could put any eligible candidate it chose into office, and the fact that it has not is the result of a highly conscious decision on the part of MCDC leaders. Indeed, they have on several occasions supported white candidates against Negroes.

As one of the leaders put it, Tuskegee Negroes want to avoid taking actions that will look like a Negro 'takeover.' MCDC leaders consider very seriously the impact that the experience of Tuskegee will

[10] See p. 32 for an explanation of 'single-shot' or 'bullet' voting.

have on other Alabama communities and the state as a whole. They want to mitigate the fear that white voters have of Negro votes. Although they are a majority in Tuskegee, they foresee that Negroes will always be a minority in statewide elections and in the vast majority of localities in the state. They hope to avoid pushing (or keeping) white voters into a bloc against Negroes. They hope that by supporting white candidates who clearly indicate their willingness to cooperate with Negroes in a situation of complete equality, they will avoid alienating whites. They see that they will be on the losing side of any statewide definition of issues as white versus black. Consequently they have not supported Negro candidates in all of the elections since Negroes became a majority.

Not all Tuskegee Negroes agree with this strategy. The MCDC and its leaders have received the most Negro abuse for their lukewarm support of Lucius Amerson, Alabama's first Negro sheriff since Reconstruction. While the MCDC never endorsed Amerson's white opponent, the most prominent leaders were far less than delighted when he ran. They viewed him as a johnny-come-lately and felt that the time was not yet right for a Negro sheriff, in that whites would not tolerate it. Some argued that his election might lead to a breakdown of law and order, at least partly because he might be sabotaged by the governor and the state police. Thus far, Amerson's detractors were wrong.

FAIR AND EQUAL TREATMENT BY LAW ENFORCEMENT AGENCIES

Justice in the United States has long been something different for Negroes than it has for whites. Crime against Negroes has been treated more leniently than crime against whites, and lawbreaking by Negroes has been handled differently from lawbreaking by whites—both more and less leniently, depending on the situation. Negroes have also suffered a disproportionate amount of police brutality.[11]

POLICE BRUTALITY. Surely the most offensive variety of police brutality is the kind of savage beating sometimes resulting in death, which is inflicted to punish Negroes for being "uppity." Other forms include several dimensions of overzealousness in the enforcement of laws, such as bullying, use of excessive counterforce, police officers taking punish-

[11] See U. S., Commission on Civil Rights, *Report,* Vol. V, *Justice* (Washington, D. C.: U. S. Government Printing Office, 1961); and U. S., Commission on Civil Rights, *Law Enforcement: A Report on Equal Protection in the South* (Washington, D. C.: U. S. Government Printing Office, 1965).

ment into their own hands, and infringement of Constitutional rights in initial contact and arrest, and in search and seizure. ("Gentlemen cops don't solve crimes.")[12]

The first kind of brutality has not been a problem in either Durham or Tuskegee. In cities that include a Negro bank, insurance company, college presidents and a Negro director of a large Veterans Administration hospital, as well as many well-paid middle class employees of those institutions, Negroes will hardly be harassed by police for buying a new car or wearing a white shirt and tie. Durham and Tuskegee simply do not have that kind of closed society, and consequently yield no evidence on the role of the vote in eliminating it. Although neither Durham nor Tuskegee has suffered systematic patterns of other forms of police brutality, there have been incidents in both cities which led to allegations of brutality against Negroes, but none have led to the conviction of the officers involved.[13] Because so few accusations are reported and because even the ones that are almost invariably involve disputed facts about what actually happened, I will make no attempt to systematically measure changes in the occurrence of brutality in order to relate them to the growth of Negro voting. The two cities yield no clear evidence on the matter, although if we were to take the accusations of brutality more seriously than the denials, we might conclude that Negro voting is not sufficient to eliminate brutality.[14] The commonness of police brutality in the ghettos of northern cities would seem to make this a safe statement.

Students of other situations have noticed a relationship between Negro voting and a decline of brutality, however, and the vote could be a mechanism for change.[15] When law enforcement is supervised by an elected official, like a sheriff, rather than an appointed police chief, Negro votes give him everything to gain and virtually nothing to lose

[12] See U. S., Commission on Civil Rights, *Justice, op. cit.,* ch. 1.

[13] See *Tuskegee News,* April 21, 1966; Harry J. Walker, "Changes in Race Accommodations in a Southern Community," (Unpublished Ph.D. dissertation, University of Chicago,1945),pp. 281-83; *The Carolina Times* (Durham), June 8, July 13, 1963, February 22, 29, September 12, November 21, 1964, October 2, 1945, May 7, 28, June 11, 1966; *Durham Morning Herald,* May 31, October 21, November 22, 1966. (Each date does not represent a separate incident.)

[14] One Durhamite I interviewed argued that police brutality declined, partly because white landlords got tired of having the doors broken down on the homes they rented to Negroes.

[15] See Clubok, *et al., op. cit.,* pp. 120-4; Holloway, *op. cit.,* p. 549; Myrdal, *op. cit.,* pp. 497-504; Whitaker, *op. cit.,* pp. 66-77,100-2,166- 67; and U. S., Commission on Civil Rights, *Voting, op. cit.,* pp. 179-82. However, for a contrary view, see Gosnell, *loc. cit.* See also U. S., Commission on Civil Rights, *Justice, op. cit.,* ch. 1.

by ceasing brutality.[16] There is less to be gained by its perpetrators and by the white community from police brutality than from some other forms of discrimination. Usually, pure wantonness yields only the crudest psychic benefits. There is no monetary cost to the white community in ceasing brutality, and one would expect that the psychic cost is minimal.

Thus ceasing brutality to gain Negro votes is not particularly likely to bring a concomitant loss of white votes. Indeed, it may even gain white votes. The Negro voter may have an important ally in the middle class white voters who may be almost as segregationist as the sheriffs accused of administering brutality. Just as white voters can help Negroes defeat race-baiters like the George Wallace-style school board candidate mentioned above (pp. 42-43), white voters may help defeat a Sheriff Screws, a Bull Connor or a Jim Clark. Because whites are more offended by some forms of discrimination than others, they are more likely to join Negroes against a brutal lawman than against candidates who do no more than give Negroes inferior and segregated public services. Negroes do not have to be a majority of voters, nor do white voters have to be liberals in the ordinary sense of the word to vote against a Bull Connor. If a contest is close between a candidate who is likely to use or condone wanton police brutality and one who is not, Negro votes may make the difference. Still, lest the differences between such candidates be over-estimated, remember Fred Shuttlesworth's remark that Albert Boutwell, the heralded moderate who defeated Bull Connor for mayor of Birmingham, was "just a dignified Bull Connor." King calls him a "consistent segregationist."[17]

REPRESENTATION ON JURIES. An important factor in equalizing the judicial treatment of Negroes is the increasing representation of Negroes on juries. There have been increases in the number of Negroes on jury lists in both cities, but the vote played a minor role if it was important at all. In Tuskegee, the change from a jury list with no Negroes to one predominantly Negro was the abrupt result of a court order, and there is no reason to attribute any element of the change to Negro voting.

---

[16] The arguments that votes will lead to a reduction of police brutality to some extent assumes that the persons responsible for law enforcement are elected, like county sheriffs, rather than appointed, like city police chiefs. However, the incidents reported in Durham and Tuskegee have often involved the sheriff's office. Probably the most important single factor combatting brutality is the professionalization of law enforcement agencies. Such professionalization is likely to be greater in more urbanized police forces than in usually more informal and personalized sheriff's departments. On the other hand, urban slum and ghetto conditions may foster more 'natural' hostility and potential violence between resident and lawman than the more personalized patterns in rural areas.

[17] Martin Luther King, *Why We Can't Wait* (New York: Signet Books, 1964), p. 59.

In Durham, the change was a much more gradual one; Negroes first appeared on juries there in the thirties, before Negro voting was significant and probably as a result of the famed Scottsboro cases, one of which threw out the rape convictions of several Negro boys because Negroes had been systematically excluded from their jury.[18] Still, the occasional Negro thought necessary to avoid appeals because of systematic exclusion became more and more common until now it is probable that the number of Negroes on juries in Durham is proportionate to their number on the tax list, from which the jury lists are drawn, although not proportionate to their number in the population.

While this information would seem to match Durham to the Tuskegee situation where litigation was important and voting unimportant to putting Negroes on juries, the situation in Durham is more complicated. After the first Negroes appeared on juries in Durham, Negroes went before the county commissioners many times requesting that Negroes be put on juries regularly. Their persistence before this elected board may have played a role in eliminating this discrimination. The problem now seems to be one of persuading Negroes selected for jury duty not to try to be excused.

TREATMENT BY THE COURTS. Informants in both Durham and Tuskegee see improvements in the way Negroes are treated in court. No doubt the increasing number of Negroes on juries in both places has helped account for this. Tuskegee Negroes, however, are not out of the woods yet. For example, in January of 1966 a white service station attendant shot and killed a young Tuskegee Negro with whom he had on several occasions shared ill feelings and sharp words. With Macon County's predominantly Negro jury lists, there was a good chance of conviction, because the accused did not deny having shot the youth, although he did plead not guilty by reason of insanity. Attorneys for the defendant successfully requested a change of venue because they said that he could not get a fair trial in Macon County. An all white jury in adjacent Lee County found the defendant not guilty of either second degree murder or first degree manslaughter. The defense depended heavily on the defendant's own testimony, and that of three persons who told of previous instances when the victim had "harassed" the defendant, as well as on sixteen character witnesses, who testified that the defendant had a "good" reputation.[19]

In Durham the improvements have included elimination of separate Bibles for swearing in, integration of seating in the courtroom, use of

[18] *Norris v. Alabama,* 294 U. S. 587 (1935).
[19] *Tuskegee News,* December 15, 1966.

"mister," "miss," etc., in addressing Negroes, and integration of the rest-rooms in the courthouse. No longer do Negroes necessarily receive inferior legal consideration, or is the testimony of Negroes necessarily admitted to evidence with a discount factor.

Negro voting may be a factor here, in that both judges and clerks are elected. As in the case of police brutality, the psychic and monetary costs to the officials or to the white community of eliminating unfair treatment of Negroes in court are probably low. The incentives to appeal or respond to Negro votes by treating Negroes more fairly might well outweigh such costs. Nevertheless, Durham experience shows that it would be a mistake to conclude that clerks and judges would immediately respond to Negro votes in such a fashion. Rather, traditional practices such as segregated seating and the avoidance of "mister" to address Negroes are supported by the force of habit.[20] The opportunity to appeal for Negro voting support or the prospect of losing such support will often not be apparent to the official, and will need to be brought to his attention in the form of a demand or a *de facto* change. Then he may respond appropriately. In Durham, for example, segregated court-room seating was eliminated when several Negroes simply began sitting in the white section. Nothing was said and the old custom slowly died out. Some observers argue that the prospect of losing Negro votes restrained court officials from preserving the status quo, but it is important to note that they did not initiate changes in order to attract Negro votes.

These remarks have a bearing on our more general understanding of the nature of the impact of the votes of Negroes or any other group on public policy. It is by no means automatic that officials who need votes to secure their positions will show great imagination and initiative in earning such votes. Perhaps the possibility of creating a backlash is sufficiently compelling to cautious public officials that they will often respond to demands but not initiate the changes themselves.[21] Perhaps they are more compelled by the prospects of losing Negro votes to another candidate than of gaining Negro votes on an issue that Negroes have not shown much concern about. Whether universally true of white southern officials or not, responsiveness to the interests of potential supporters at least constitutes a dimension on which elected officials will vary.

As in so many policy outputs discussed in this book, there are other important influences on the improved ways in which Negroes are

[20] I am indebted to Richard McCleery for emphasizing to me the importance of habit in political life.
[21] See V. O. Key, Jr., *Public Opinion and American Democracy* (New York, Alfred A. Knopf, 1961), p. 424, for an excellent statement on this matter.

treated in courts. One is the growing willingness of the federal courts to reverse or remand cases which involve discrimination and the accompanying willingness of Negroes to appeal on such grounds. Both Durham and Tuskegee Negroes have been in court on racial matters almost continuously since the forties, and both have appealed cases all the way to the U. S. Supreme Court. The prospect of appeal is probably not lost on Durham and Tuskegee judges.

EQUAL DISTRIBUTION OF PUBLIC SERVICES
DIRECTLY AFFECTING THE HOUSEHOLD

One important thing that city governments do for their citizens is to provide a number of concrete services that are enjoyed on the household level. They include streets, curbs, gutters, water, sewers and garbage collection, as well as enforcement of housing codes. The distribution of these services in Durham and Tuskegee illustrates an important point about the utility of the Negro vote, specifically that the procedures a city has established to govern the distribution of services will have an important bearing on the prospects that votes will bring a fair distribution of them. In Tuskegee, for example, street paving in Negro areas was one of the most striking results of Negro enfranchisement, while in Durham, years of cohesive and maneuverable Negro voting have left a great many unpaved streets in the Negro sections of that city.

STREET PAVING. In Tuskegee all of the streets in white sections had been paved before Negro enfranchisement, whereas Negro sections were substantially worse off. After Negroes became a majority of the voters even the *ancien régime* yielded to political realities and paved five ' Negro streets, ' though an official of the new administration avers that they did a substandard job and left it to their successors to pay for them. The new administration has paved over fifteen more Negro streets and at the time of this writing had firm plans to cover all remaining dirt streets within a year or less. All the newly paved streets receive curbs, gutters and drive aprons at no cost.

This was one of the most obvious inequities of the old system, and a natural basis for appealing to Negro votes. It seems as if the old regime was making a belated effort to make up for a few of the past injustices. The new administration has demonstrated that it is serious about changing the old order, and apparently saw that this is an important step in that direction which would be hard to overlook. There is no doubt that the change in voting patterns is the root cause of the new paving policy.

In Durham, on the other hand, there is little in the way of paved streets to show for Negro votes. A casual drive through almost any of the Negro areas in Durham will reveal a great many streets without paving, gutters or curbs. The city demonstrates that cohesive and maneuverable voting of a large bloc of Negroes is no guarantee of such city services, but the reason is not that in spite of the Negro vote the city discriminates against Negroes by neglecting to provide for them what they provide for other residents. The crucial fact is that in Durham, unlike Tuskegee, citizens have to pay for their own street paving.

Durham city government does not directly assume the cost for paving all city streets. Paving is paid for by the people who own property on the street in question. The resources necessary for paving in Durham do not include political influence so much as money and the ability to persuade one's neighbors that they too should help pay. As a rule, Durham's streets are paved by petition. Under this procedure, one must persuade over 50 percent of the property owners representing over 50 percent of the frontage on a given street to sign a petition to have the street paved. If this requirement is fulfilled, all owners on the street, whether they signed the petition or not, are assessed for the paving according to their frontage. The city contracts for the job to be done. If the cost is less than the designated sum per foot, the city charges at cost, but if the cost is more than that sum, the city absorbs the loss.

The basic form of politics here is that of persuading one's neighbors that they should pave the street. A successful petition goes before the city council, which sets a date for a hearing so any objections may be raised, but it is rare that anyone does object. There is virtually no room for political pull here.[22] If you and your neighbors want the paving and have the money, you have it done. If you do not want to or cannot afford to, it does not get done. It is not a matter of race, but of economics.[23]

The same patterns prevail in the distribution of water and sewer facilities. In Durham, citizens must bear the cost of laying water and

[22] Streets may be paved by enabling act, which involves a little more politics. The city can order major thoroughfares or connecting links to be paved even though a majority of the owners representing over half the frontage do not agree. Someone who cannot secure the cooperation of his neighbors may conceivably use some political influence to get the city council to order a street paved under this procedure, but it does not happen very often. Even in this sort of situation the owners pay at the set rate according to their frontage. Political persuasion may overcome the resistance of one's neighbors, but it will not overcome the necessity to bear the cost. While some Negroes claim credit for Durham's adoption of the enabling act procedure, even this does not change the basic situation wherein voting is almost totally irrelevant to street paving.
[23] The economics of the situation for the Negro often involves a landlord, who may be white or Negro.

sewer lines, and the vote has been virtually irrelevant. In Tuskegee, the city bears the cost, and improvements have been made by the new administration as a result of Negro voting.

GARBAGE COLLECTION is a household related public service which is provided to all citizens in both cities as a matter of right, with the cost being borne by the city. As in street paving, Negro votes provided striking changes in Tuskegee, where there was a lot of improvement to be made. Before the Negro voting majority discrimination was rampant. Some areas had their garbage picked up three times a week, some once, and some never. Some residents had to bring their garbage out to the street for collection and others did not. Negroes invariably received the shoddier service. Since Negro voting replaced city administrations, service has been equal. The process is obvious enough. Negro voting was instrumental in replacing an old administration that discriminated against Negroes with a new one that is scrupulous in responding to Negro grievances and in treating Negroes and whites fairly. In fact, one Negro resident of Tuskegee claims that when he called the mayor to tell him that dogs were knocking over his garbage cans before the collectors came, the mayor sent the police over to collect the garbage! Durham, unfortunately, yields no clear evidence about the impact of Negro voting on garbage collection.

HOUSING CODES. Housing is one of the Negro's severest problems. Residential segregation keeps Negroes from moving into desirable neighborhoods that they can afford, and lack of available housing for Negroes forces overcrowding and inordinate demand for the substandard housing available in the ghetto. In the absence of the incentives that go along with a completely open housing market, rents go up and standards of maintenance go down, compounding the problems of the slum dweller. Housing codes are well suited to alleviate or mitigate these problems by forcing landlords to maintain minimum standards in the dwellings they rent.

Durham has had an operating housing code since 1949. It was revised in 1963 and supplemented with a seven year enforcement program. The 1960 U. S. Census reported that 22 percent of the housing in Durham was deteriorated (in need of more repair than would be required for regular maintenance) or dilapidated (not providing safe and adequate shelter). Much of this was and is in several Negro slums, and its very existence was evidence that a cohesive and deliverable Negro vote had not been sufficient to remove it. The city reported in 1963 that over 7,000 buildings had been brought into compliance since 1949, but, as it recognized, a great many remained in need of improvement. The seven year enforcement program was designed to bring all housing up to standard.[24] While all of the city's housing was included in the program, some areas were given lower priority than others. Among those receiving low priority are both the very best areas which are least in need of enforcement, and also some of the very worst areas, which are in greatest need, but which also are scheduled for razing by urban renewal.

Housing code enforcement has been a sensitive issue in Durham since 1965 when a number of dwellings in one of the slums were bought by a new landowner who raised rents without making any improvements in the houses, which were below minimum housing code standards to begin with. Since then Durham Negroes have appeared repeatedly before the city council seeking housing code enforcement and have resorted to picketing landowners and realtors. The extent and effectiveness of code enforcement remain at issue between a good many Negroes on the one hand, and landowners and the city government on the other. While the city's building inspector acknowledges that houses that are brought up to minimum standard do not always stay there, his position is that the code has ultimately been enforced in all cases in which it has been applied. In no case has the city used its last recourse of going to court to apply a fifty dollar per day fine to the landowner for each day he fails to bring his dwelling into compliance, although it has granted repeated extensions to its deadlines.

Many Negroes, on the other hand, simply do not agree that the city is adequately enforcing its housing code. As of this writing, during the Detroit riots of July, 1967, Negroes have marched on city hall twice within a week following a city council meeting attended by more than 150 Negroes, some of whom threatened that Durham is not immune to being another Watts, Newark or Vietnam. During one of the marches the National Guard was called out. Subsequent to these events the city council appointed a five-man committee to help solve some of the housing and other grievances.

After negotiations with United Organizations for Community Improvement (UOCI), the spearhead of Negro demands, the city council committee agreed to recommend, among other things, "enforcement of the housing code to the letter—even if it means eviction into the street. . . . Hiring additional Negroes in the building inspection division. (and) . . . Expediting inspection matters by proposing a revamped system."[25] The controversy remains unresolved, but even if all Negro housing code enforcement demands are met, just how much of the gains can be linked directly to the Negro vote is not clear. The present council may

[24] See "A Seven Year Housing Code Enforcement Program for the City of Durham" (City of Durham, mimeo, December, 1963).
[25] *Durham Morning Herald*, July 22, 1967.

be more responsive to Negro demands than one which was not selected with the help of Negro votes, but avoiding the conclusion that racial tension in Durham and elsewhere in the nation expedited the response is difficult.

In Tuskegee, the housing code issue has been expressed in a very different fashion. There has been an ordinance in that city which required that new construction and major remodeling could not be begun without the consent of the owners of property surrounding the lot to be built on. The rationale for this ordinance included not only considerations of maintaining an esthetically pleasing neighborhood, but also the inevitable mechanism for prohibiting Negroes from building in a previously all white neighborhood. Apparently some Negroes already living in white neighborhoods were denied permits to remodel their homes by their neighbors, who hoped that the Negroes' homes would come so near to collapsing as to be totally unlivable, thus forcing the Negro family to move away! This ordinance was rigidly enforced previous to 1964. After the Negro vote had replaced the old regime, the U. S. Forest Service wanted to build a home for the ranger at a nearby forest. Several prospective neighbors of the federal employee objected to granting the Government a permit, because they felt that Washington might someday appoint a Negro forest ranger. The new city council had the alternative of repealing the ordinance or denying the Government's application. They chose the former.

Both the Durham and Tuskegee experiences in the housing matters illustrate a point I have made earlier and will make again—that even when Negro voting is a relevant and useful resource, it does not necessarily work automatically. Officials who are elected with the help of Negro votes often need some prodding, even if they are self-consciously interested in doing right by the Negro community. Even if, as in Tuskegee, they are unusually committed to bringing about a system of complete equality, they may not be *aware* of all of the inequities. Thus it is often necessary for citizens to petition the government to alleviate particular grievances, partly just to inform them of the demands, and partly to put the pressure on. Some elected officials may be so solicitous of votes as to seek out opportunities to meet the needs of groups in the population. Most southern local officials are not quite so aggressive in soliciting Negro votes. Further, in cities such as Durham with white majorities, the advantages of doing so are not without some disadvantages for the elected benefactors.

To some degree city governments in these two cities depend on Negro elected officials to articulate the interests of the Negro community. Indeed, this is an obvious reason why direct Negro representation is important on the councils. In both cities, the Negro councilmen have been middle class, including businessmen, college professors and a minister. These men are in a far higher economic bracket than rank and file Negroes in either city. They themselves may not be overly conscious of the conditions in which many of the Negroes they represent live. Even if they are aware, they do not personally endure the sorts of living conditions that would make them as personally interested in improving some matters as they might be.[26] This suggests two things. One is that it may be desirable for lower strata Negroes to have direct representation on bodies like city councils. The other is that even if this is not feasible for whatever reason, indirect representation by whites or higher status Negroes may be supplemented by direct presentation or grievances when they exist by those who experience them. Even if the indirect representatives are aggressive proponents of lower class Negro interests, their hand can be strengthened and their influence enhanced by direct presentation of grievances. In this sense the neighborhood councils in Durham which are supported by the North Carolina Fund and the Office of Economic Opportunity are very valuable supplements to the Negro vote.

OTHER PUBLIC SERVICES DISTRIBUTED BY LOCAL GOVERNMENT

Negro votes may affect the distribution of other public services besides those which directly affect the household. The experience of Durham Negroes in improving their recreation facilities and fire protection illustrates the point that bond issue elections may be an especially useful channel of Negro voting influence.

RECREATION FACILITIES. The Negro vote has played a significant role in both cities in improving the recreation facilities available to Negroes. In Tuskegee, the change follows the pattern described in street paving and garbage collection: it was quite clearly and directly the result of Negro votes effecting a change in administration.

There are two main parks in Tuskegee, each with a swimming pool and a community building. Both were segregated before the Keever administration took over in 1964, and integrated by the new council. The new policy was strongly resented by numerous whites, and acid and excrement were dumped into the pools. Because of the tensions over the issue and because of the prospect of the same thing happening to the pools repeatedly throughout the season, the pools were not reopened

---

[26] For an exaggeratedly uncharitable interpretation of middle class Negro political leaders, see E. Franklin Frazier, *Black Bourgeoisie* (Glencoe, Ill.: The Free Press, 1957), ch. 4, especially pp. 86, 105, 109.

until the following year. There have been no incidents since then, and the decision of the Keever council to integrate has been effective.

In Durham, the situation is more complicated, but the Negro vote was important there as well as in Tuskegee in securing improvements. There were really two issues in Durham, rather than one simple integration question. Negro sections of the city had had their own recreation facilities for many years, so the question of fair and equal distribution of such facilities between Negro and white residential areas had to be faced, as well as that of integration. The two issues were faced separately.

While all city recreation facilities are now integrated in Durham, most parks are still used predominantly by members of only one race, because of residential segregation. The fourteen parks used mostly by whites are evaluated at $913,000 while the nine parks frequented most often by Negroes are evaluated at $442,000. This appears to be a fairly equitable distribution, since the 'Negro parks' constitute 33 percent of the valuation of parks used by only one race, and Negroes constitute 36 percent of the city population. Forest Hills Park, the city's largest, is used commonly by both races. It is valued at $300,000 and in practice is as accessible to Negroes as the parks used predominantly by Negroes. The distribution of such facilities as baseball diamonds, tennis courts, swimming pools and community centers between the white and Negro parks is for the most part quite fair and equitable if population distribution is used as a basis for evaluation.[27]

The general picture then, is that Negroes are currently treated fairly in Durham's system of public recreation. Of course there are still complaints that the number and quality of facilities in Negro areas are still inadequate. This appears to be true, but seems also true of white sections. One also hears that Negro facilities are inferior to those in white areas, but there is dispute over this even among the Negroes.

This more or less equitable situation is unquestionably a substantial improvement over that existing twenty to twenty-five years ago before the Negro vote was very sizeable or well organized. While no concrete time series data are available, white and Negro alike acknowledge that Negroes are treated much more fairly in recreation facilities than before. This is not by any means to argue that we can wholly account for this change with Negro voting, but I do contend that the Negro vote played an important role, and that the process through which it had its effect can be identified.

The crucial channel of influence is the bond issue election. It is

[27] For further details see William R. Keech, "The Negro Vote as a Political Resource: The Case of Durham" (Unpublished Ph.D. dissertation, University of Wisconsin, 1966), pp. 130-3.

important because it appears to give Negroes a more direct influence on a number of policies than they have on most policies not subject to bond issue influence. Two characteristics of bond issue elections make them especially responsive to Negro voting. One is that the proposals are invariably made by someone who wants them to win, which is of course the purpose of proposing them. Secondly, they are by their very nature issue elections in a way that elections of candidates for office are not.

The concern of bond issue proponents that their proposal win and be funded makes them particularly sensitive to opposition, and responsive to the demands of groups that may be in a position to provide a margin of defeat. The issue orientation matter is slightly more subtle. One of the reasons the Negro vote has not been successful in many areas is that the process through which it must take effect is through influencing candidate elections which often involve issues only marginally if at all. Even if there are important issues involved, they are often obscured in hazy distinctions between candidates. This is probably even more true of non-partisan elections such as those for city council in these two cities than in partisan elections.[28] Candidates often obscure or play down issues intentionally, especially when they agree, which is not uncommon. This is particularly true of racial issues in a city like Durham where Negroes are a minority and it is not an electoral advantage among whites to be identified with Negro interests.

Thus, in candidate elections, Negroes often find no alternative which is clearly preferable for them. Issues in candidate elections are often not sufficiently clear cut for a deliverable vote to have a very good chance of influencing the behavior of the aspirant for office. A bond issue election, in contrast, is really a referendum on an issue. The issue is relatively clear and placed directly before the voters. Bond issue proponents are likely to be responsive to whatever aspects of the proposal are made salient to them by the demands of a sizeable group of voters. When voting support is made contingent on the more equitable distribution of the bond-supported facilities, the proponents of the bond issue are somewhat more vulnerable than a candidate who is not so directly tied to a particular distribution of facilities, or who can postpone a commitment.

Also an issue like the distribution of recreation facilities between white and Negro areas is not especially likely to become salient in a candidate election. In an election for recreation bonds, on the other hand, there is no obscuring of the recreation issue. It is the *raison d'être*

[28] See Charles Adrian, "Some General Characteristics of Non-partisan Elections," *American Political Science Review,* XLVI(1952),pp. 766-76, especially pp. 772-73.

of the election. If the bond issue proponents perceive that Negroes might oppose the bonds on the grounds that the facilities they will pay for are to be segregated or inequitably distributed between white and Negro residential areas, they may well make an adjustment to improve chances of victory.

Through exactly this sort of process recreation facilities have become more fairly distributed to Durham Negroes. There have been five bond issue elections since 1945 which have dealt in some degree with recreation facilities. The DCNA supported four of them and opposed one. The four they supported (1947, 1954, 1959, and 1965) won, while the one they opposed (1951) lost. The 1951 issue was opposed because Negro leaders felt that the funds were not to be equitably distributed between whites and Negroes.

This description slightly overestimates the power of the Negro vote to settle bond elections. The 1951 issue probably would have lost anyway.[29] The 1947 and 1959 issues would have been defeated if the Negro precincts had reversed themselves. The 1954 bonds and permission tax could not have been defeated with the reversal of the Negro precincts alone, although Negro votes from other precincts might have been able to make it possible. Unfortunately we do not know exactly how many of the Negro voters were unaccounted for by the Negro precincts. The same thing is true of the 1965 bond issue, but in this case it is even more unlikely that there would have been sufficient Negro votes outside of the Negro precincts.

Still, whatever the actual importance of the Negro vote in deciding a given bond election, it is likely to be perceived as important in Durham. The probable outcome of a bond election is rarely known with **any certainty**, and aggressive proponents are likely to want to co-opt as much of the potential opposition as they can without compromising the values they seek with the bond issue itself.

More money for parks in Negro areas is just the kind of marginal adjustment that bond issue advocates can usually make without compromising those values. Also, marginal adjustments are unlikely to be very visible and controversial to the white public. In short they are easy concessions for bond issue proponents to make. Just how many of the facilities actually allocated to Negro areas in Durham since 1945 would have gone there without this bargaining strength is not known, but a strong case can be made that the vote has been important in insuring a fair distribution.

While bond elections are an important channel of influence, they

[29] Even if the Negro precincts had gone for the issue in the same proportions they tallied against it, it would have been defeated.

too do not automatically provide equal distribution of services supported by the bonds. The forces of habit support the shortchanging of Negroes in the distribution of many public facilities. I have already argued that politicians often lack imagination and initiative in appealing for Negro votes; it is important for Negroes to make their grievances and demands known. Recreation has been one of the things that Durham's middle class Negro leadership has concerned itself with. A more equitable distribution of parks is something they can demand or request without threatening the accommodating relationships they have with Durham's white political leaders.

Integration of parks was a somewhat tougher nut to crack than fair distribution. Integration is more visible and salient to the white population. Negro voting was not particularly instrumental in integrating Durham parks. Negro leaders did play an important role in securing that integration, but the prospect of litigation and losing a costly court suit seems to have been more important than votes.

Up to 1957 there was no integration of any recreation facilities to speak of in Durham. In that year, Negroes got permission to use the tennis courts at the then white Forest Hills Park for a Negro tournament. Soon thereafter, some Negroes tried to use the courts for private play and were ejected. Several of the most prominent Negro leaders conferred with the mayor, city manager and police chief and the group worked out the compromise that Negroes would make no mass moves to use the white recreation facilities, while those Negroes using them would no longer be ejected. The city attorney had advised city officials that there was no constitutional basis for maintaining segregation in these facilities. DCNA leadership is far more aggressive in litigation than in the use of other resources, and this fact cannot have been lost on the officials. At the same time, the Negro leadership was asking little enough that concessions were fairly easy for the officials to make—certainly less risk for them than more striking changes.

The next time integration came up as an issue in public recreation was in 1961, when a day camp was planned at Lake Michie, a city owned park near Durham. There was to be a two-week camp program for white youngsters and a one-week program for Negroes. The Recreation Advisory Committee was persuaded by its two Negro members to reverse its position and to have no restrictions on attendance of Negroes at the camp. Applications were to be accepted on a first-come-first-served basis. There were no repercussions from running an integrated camp.

In 1963 the more sensitive question of integrating the pools came before the Recreation Advisory Committee. A decision was reached with the city manager and the city attorney to recommend the integration of the pools. Negroes attempting to swim in white pools up to that point had been turned away. A number of neighborhood groups had requested of the recreation director that the pools be opened, and the director brought the issue before the advisory committee. Though no pressure was brought to the city officials, apparently there would have been a suit had the pools not been opened voluntarily. Were it not for federal law, no doubt many of these advances would have been made more slowly. There was no particular point at which other facilities like picnic areas and so forth were integrated. Negroes began using all the recreation facilities but the pools about 1962, and there was no opposition. They were permitted to go ahead, certainly for reasons similar to those cited above.

FIRE PROTECTION. Tuskegee is a small enough city that one fire station serves the whole city. The only possibility for discrimination in fire protection is that the fire department might pay less attention to calls from Negroes than from whites. This has not been a source of complaint.

Durham, in contrast, is large enough to need several stations, which may or may not adequately cover Negro residential areas. In the past, these sections have been shortchanged. While fire protection in Hayti, the main Negro section, is still said to be inferior and on a lower level than that in other areas of the city, clearly it has improved, and the improvement is directly attributable in part to the Negro vote—through the same bond issue process cited above.

For some time during the 1940's, Durham Negroes complained about the fact that they were not served by a fire station very close to most of the homes in Hayti and because there were no Negro firemen. In the spring of 1950 a number of prominent Negroes representing the DCNA appeared before the city council to voice this complaint and to request an adjustment. About a year later a series of bond issue questions including one for fire station bonds (for the whole city) was presented to the voters. The DCNA endorsed all of the bond issues with the understanding that one of the new stations would be in the Hayti section and that it would be manned by Negro firemen.

This particular bond won by 1211 votes. Eighty-four percent of the votes in the all Negro precincts went in favor of the bond issue, giving it a margin of 1,181 votes, or just thirty less than the margin of victory. The issue certainly would have lost if the DCNA had opposed it. In any case it did win with a significant assist from Negro votes, and a Negro manned fire station for Hayti was in the works. In view of the earlier analysis of the recreation issue, the assistance of Negro votes must be seen not only as helping effect the victory of the bond issue as it stood, but also as helping to secure an alternative that included a Negro manned fire station for Hayti.

Negro voting support was probably more crucial on the question of hiring Negro firemen than on the location of a new station in Hayti. Fire insurance rates for the whole city are adjusted in accordance with recommendations of the National Fire Underwriters. Rates go up when a large area is badly protected, as was the case in Hayti and several other sections. Thus, the standards of the underwriters must be considered along with the Negro vote as one of the causes for improvement of the standards of fire protection for Negroes.

LIBRARIES. In libraries as in so many other things, the racial questions for analysis in Tuskegee are much simpler than they are in Durham. During the long dry period for Negroes before 1964 there was no library at all in either Tuskegee or Macon County—for either Negro or white. The one that has been built since then is, of course, integrated.

For years Durham has had two separate library systems, each with a separate budget and governing board. While in the past one was for Negroes and the other for whites, they are both now integrated and in the process of merger. The physical plant of the Negro library is superior to that of the white in many respects, but this difference should not be attributed to voting strength. More important is the fact that Negro citizens over the years have taken a special interest in their library and have made substantial gifts to it. A private corporation serves it. Its funds come not only from these private sources, but also from the city, the county and the state.

The integration of the white library, like that of the parks, was not directly related to Negro voting. The white library was informally segregated until 1959. At that time, a young Negro minister simply began to use it and, while there was tension, there were no incidents. The number of Negroes using this library slowly increased, but Negroes were never turned away or prohibited from using the facilities, although they were discriminated against in subtler ways. By 1964, even these subtler forms of mistreatment had been eliminated. Negroes are treated like other patrons in every respect. In fact, the library has hired a Negro girl to work part time at the desk. The Negro vote seems to have played no role in these changes. Officials knew there were inevitable changes going on. They had been advised by the city attorney that there was no constitutional basis for preserving segregation in such facilities, and that they would be vulnerable to lawsuit if they tried to block changes.

CEMETERIES. In Tuskegee, the *ancien régime* reacted after their defeat to the prospect that the new administration would integrate the city's white cemetery by selling it after the election but before the new council took office. Thus when the Keever administration took over the city owned no cemeteries. The incident well illustrates the intransigence of Tuskegee elected officials before Negroes became a voting majority.

In Durham the question of cemetery integration was resolved recently (early 1967) when a white city councilman asked that the city repeal sections of the city code which segregated the two city owned cemeteries, which it did. The city attorney had advised him that the code restrictions were in conflict with federal law. A white councilman rather than the (then single) Negro on the council requested the change, in spite of the fact that the Negro councilman had earlier told me that he was aware that the city cemeteries were segregated. The Negro community's representatives on the city council have not always been notably aggressive in seeking elimination of all forms of discrimination.

PUBLIC SERVICES DIRECTLY INFLUENCED BY STATE AND FEDERAL POLICIES

Local officials do not always have a free hand in administering local affairs. Sometimes this is because of increasing Federal control over something that has traditionally been a state or local function, like public schools or hospitals. Otherwise, it may be because a program was originally begun at the initiative of the federal government, like public housing. In either case, what impact local Negro voting has on them is desirable to know.

SCHOOL INTEGRATION is one of the most critical areas for Negro advancement. The type of education that Negroes receive has an important bearing on whether or not they will be able to break out of the cycle of poverty and ghetto living that closes off so many opportunities. Education is crucially important for the development of the skills and self-esteem that are necessary to compete for jobs and for equal opportunity to enjoy the advantages of society. If the vote enabled Negroes to break out of their separate and unequal schools, it would open one of the most promising channels for Negro advancement. Unfortunately it did not do so in either Durham or Tuskegee.

In both cities, integration of the schools was the more or less direct result of litigation, rather than voting. This fact is especially clear in Tuskegee, where the desegregation was directly pursuant to a court order. The initial integration created such a reaction that real integration was not effected until later. After the local school board had ignored Governor Wallace's command that they disobey the federal court order to integrate the schools in 1963, the governor sent some 150-200 state troopers to "stand in the schoolhouse door." The school was closed temporarily, but a few weeks later it reopened with thirteen Negro students and fourteen white teachers. The bulk of the white students attended the newly constituted Macon Academy which was immediately organized as a direct result of the "integration" of the public school, and enjoyed the financial support of the governor.[30] By the 1964-65 school year, Tuskegee High School was integrated in fact as well as name, with 14 Negro and 142 white students, but the line that continues to separate those Tuskegee whites who are willing to cooperate with the Negroes in an integrated society from those who say "never" is virtually equivalent to the line that separates those who support the public schools and those who send their children to Macon Academy. When race is discussed in Tuskegee, whites are described as "public school people" or "Macon Academy people." When Negro votes were in the minority, then, they had virtually no influence over school board policy. Litigation was the key channel of influence on school board policy for Negroes.

Durham Negroes have also found the courts the most effective channel to influence education policy. The Durham city school board has consistently resisted a whole series of moves toward thorough school integration ever since segregated schools were declared unconstitutional in 1954. Durham Negroes have had the city school board in court almost continuously since 1957, and virtually every move towards further integration came about in piecemeal fashion as a result of a series of court orders. In fact, Negroes had had to go to court in 1949 to secure injunctive relief from discrimination in the distribution of segregated school facilities.[31]

While the initial integration of Durham schools was in a strict sense a voluntary decision of the school board, the pattern of litigation and other events makes it clear that it was done involuntarily and in anticipation of a court order. In June of 1955, soon after the second Brown decision and the passage of a new state pupil assignment act, the board appointed a committee to study the problems involved in desegregation. About a month later a prominent Negro leader presented the board with a statement and a petition signed by over 700 Negroes requesting reorganization of the city's school system on a nondiscriminatory basis. Yet no action was taken in that year. The committee reported on the first of August that it had not had time to complete studies of the problems rising from the Brown decision and recommended that the schools be opened in September 1955 on the

[30] In 1964, Governor Wallace gave Macon Academy $6,000 from his campaign chest. *The Tuskegee News,* September 3, 1964.
[31] See Keech, *op. cit.,* pp. 135-51 for further details on Durham schools.

same basis as before. In October of 1956, the board was again petitioned on behalf of several hundred Negroes and asked for a desegregation plan. The board advised the petitioners that its committee needed time for further study to formulate a recommendation that would "meet with sufficient public support to insure continued operation of our local public schools."[32] The first actual requests for reassignment to white schools came from nine Negroes in the summer of 1957. Later that summer the board adopted a resolution that had the effect of freezing the existing pattern of segregation. New assignments were to be made on the basis of two maps, one for whites and one for Negroes.

In rejecting all nine applications for reassignment to white schools, the board said that

it is our considered opinion that conditions and circumstances are such that any departure from former policies would result in injustice to the children of both races, and therefore, we decline the request for reassignment made by each of the following . . . . It is also our considered opinion that such a refusal will not develop harmful psychological effects to the children who have requested reassignment, but to grant such requests, or any of them would be harmful psychologically to a great many children of both races.[33]

Thus the school board was not only resolving to continue its previous practice of assigning students on the basis of racial considerations, but was explicitly rejecting the rationale for the Brown decision. When attorneys for the Negro families requested a hearing on the decision, one was held . . . . twenty-eight days after school had started, but the board simply reaffirmed its previous decision. Meanwhile the schools in Winston-Salem, Charlotte and Greensboro, which did not have the high level of Negro voting found in Durham, had peacefully and voluntarily integrated.

In March of 1958 several members of the biracial Human Relations Commission, appointed in the previous year by the city council, appeared before the school board and offered their assistance on the school segregation question. More specifically, they asked the school board to act on a request by the local NAACP to meet with the board to discuss the possibilities of integration. The school board responded to this presentation by saying nothing. When the chairman of the Human Relations Commission asked how to interpret the silence, the school board chairman reputedly advised him to interpret it simply as silence.

[32] *McKissick* v. *Durham City Board of Education,* 176 F. Supp. 3 (1959), p. 6. This suit was brought on behalf of the daughter of Floyd McKissick, now national director of CORE, then a Durham lawyer.
[33] *Ibid.,* p. 9.

Two of the Negroes who had been denied reassignment in 1957 brought suit against the city school board asking that a three judge federal court be convened to enjoin the school board from enforcing parts of the state constitution, statutes and administrative orders, which they held were contrary to the Fourteenth Amendment of the Federal Constitution in that they required segregation of the races. They also sought to have the legal rights of the class of people they represented be declared and that the court order the school board to promptly present a plan of desegregation.

The court observed that what the plaintiffs were really seeking was a general order of desegregation rather than admission as individuals to any particular school. This it refused to give. It held that the burden of proof is on the plaintiffs to establish that they had exhausted their administrative remedies under state law before applying for relief to the federal court, and that because they had failed to do this the court was not called on to determine the reasons they were denied reassignment.[34] This case was then dropped. By the time it was handed down in 1959, seven Negroes had been reassigned to formerly all white schools for the 1959-60 school year.

The first integration was in a strict sense voluntary. It did not directly result from a court order, but it is clear that the board was not doing it because it wanted to. The Negroes lost this particular case because they brought it on the wrong grounds, not because there *were* no grounds. The school board could expect that unless they yielded and admitted some Negroes, some would soon exhaust their administrative remedies and seek relief successfully in court. The failure to take action in 1955, the alleged need for further time to study the problem in 1956, the denial of petitions in 1957, the disavowal of the Brown decision, the hearing on the denial a month after school started and the silent response to the city council-appointed Human Relations Committee all reflect a clear reluctance to obey federal law. Some of the actions indicate bad faith dealings with the Negroes. Indeed, in spite of denying direct relief to the Negroes, the court felt called upon to say that it

heartily disapproved the methods employed by the Durham City Board of Education in giving assignment notices, and particularly the delay in making assignments. Some of the resolutions adopted by the Board regarding the applications of these plaintiffs strongly suggest that reassignments were denied solely because of the race and color of the applicants.[35]

[34] *Ibid.*, pp. 14-16.
[35] *Ibid.*, p. 16.

Given all of these factors, it seems reasonable to infer that the board was committed to maintaining segregation as long as it could, and that the reassignment of seven Negroes in 1959-1960 was a recognition of the handwriting on the wall—a bow to the inevitable. There is no reason to believe that the Negro votes played any role.

If we accept the argument that Negro votes were not important in integrating the schools in either city when it actually happened, does this commit us to asserting that integration is just too hot an issue to be affected by Negro votes? We would come substantially closer to this position for Durham than Tuskegee. The crucial difference is that in one city Negro votes are a minority and in the other a majority of the electorate.

School segregation has probably been the most sensitive and conflict-laden issue of the whole civil rights revolution. Probably a large majority of whites in Durham preferred to keep segregated schools.[36] Quite clearly the school board did. Opposition to school integration in the South has been at least as strong and vocal as its advocacy. If anything it has been more shrill. It seems to be a clear case of a minority of the electorate demanding what a majority adamantly refused to give. One would not expect the smaller number of voters to prevail over the larger in a situation where votes directly influenced the outcomes. The Durham situation, however, is complicated by the fact that the school board is insulated from the influence of voters by being appointed rather than elected. We would not expect Negro votes to be able to effect integration of the schools in Durham so long as they are a minority of the electorate, and so long as a larger proportion of the electorate remains firmly opposed. Further, we would not expect Negro votes to be able to secure integration as long as the school board remains firmly opposed, and so long as it is insulated from the direct influence of any voters by being appointed rather than elected.

This is not to suggest that the ability of Negro votes to integrate the schools would be enhanced in Durham by an elected school board. If anything, an elected school board in Durham might have been more adamantly opposed to integration. The effect of appointment is to insulate the board from electoral pressures. If electoral pressures to maintain segregation are stronger than those favoring integration, appoint-

[36] Durham County was one of the sampling units in Donald Matthews' and James Prothro's southwide sample surveys of Negroes and whites used in their *Negroes and the New Southern Politics* (New York: Harcourt, Brace and World, 1966). Over 60 percent of the whites in Durham County stated that they preferred segregation, while less than 20 percent preferred integration and about 20 percent were in between. The question was about segregation and integration in general, and can be found on p. 512 of their book (B-70).

ment would give the board more freedom to ignore these pressures and integrate, if it chose to do so.

Can we account for the Durham school board's opposition to integration with the role of votes? City councilmen disavow influence over school board policy, although they appoint the board and are certainly in a position to affect it. Clearly councilmen consider school policy a hot potato that they do not care to burn their fingers on. They may self-consciously appoint segregationists to the school board at the same time they disavow any hand in school policy, or there may be something about the school board itself that socializes its members to the overall segregationist posture, or perhaps both.

While in Durham the prospects are very slim that Negro votes might have secured integration without radical changes in other conditions, the situation in Tuskegee is quite different. It seems reasonable to expect that Negro votes would have been able to secure integration there if it had remained an issue after Negroes became a majority of the electorate. Two of the conditions which removed the Durham school board from the influence of Negro votes are not present in Tuskegee. First and most important, Negroes constitute a majority of the electorate, and are in a position to ultimately prevail on any issues they choose to press. The involvement of Negro leadership in litigation to integrate the schools in both communities makes it likely that the leaders in both cities would have chosen to press the issue. Secondly, the school board in Tuskegee is elected rather than appointed. There is one school board for all of Macon County, but Negroes are a majority of the county as well as the city electorate, although they are a somewhat larger majority in the city. The elected school board would be more likely to be responsive to an interested majority than a board insulated from the electorate by appointment. For these reasons, I anticipate that school policy in Tuskegee will in the future be quite responsive to Negro demands.

Durham school policy has been resistant to the impact of Negro votes even after its initial concession on integration. Litigation against the school board has gone on almost continuously since that change. The Fourth Circuit Court of Appeals found in 1962 that in spite of the fact that the school board had done away with the dual assignment maps, one for whites and one for Negroes, and "despite the board's dutiful resolution, it has continued to utilize the dual attendance areas, if not the very maps themselves, to maintain segregated schools in the city."[37]

The court's

[37] *Wheeler* v. *Durham City Board of Education,* 309 F. 2nd 630 (1962), p. 632.

inescapable conclusion from the evidence is that the assignment of pupils to the Durham public schools is based, in whole or in part, upon the race of those assigned . . . .

This opinion could go on to discuss in detail the instances, abundantly appearing in the record, of unfairness and arbitrariness in the procedures imposed upon the applicants for transfers to free themselves from the initial racial assignments. We find it unnecessary.[38]

Finally the court gave the Durham Negroes what they had been seeking all along—an order for admission to the schools to which they had applied, a declaratory judgment that the school board was administering the law in an unconstitutional manner, and an injunction against its discriminatory practices. Subsequently, three desegregation plans submitted by the board of education were rejected by the federal courts, and in 1965 the courts ordered a freedom-of-choice plan that put initial placement in the hands of the parents, rather than simply allowing them to remove their children from the discriminatory arrangements initially set up by the school board. Since then, the courts have ordered faculty integration in Durham schools as well.

This series of cases is clear evidence of the insufficiency of a Negro voting bloc of the size and maneuverability of that in Durham to secure virtually any aspect of integration. This bleak picture does not, however, mean that Negro votes in Durham have been totally irrelevant to school policy. In fact, there is one case in which they were even instrumental in integrating an industrial education center to be built there. Once again, the decisions were made pursuant to bond issue elections.

The fact that Durham has been growing more slowly than the other major North Carolina cities in the past two decades has been a matter of concern to city leaders. Because of this concern, these leaders were very eager to bring Durham one of the new technical training institutes the state was sponsoring (largely as a result of the efforts of one of Durham's representatives in the state legislature). To do this the county would have to pass a $350,000 bond issue to build it, and the Negro vote would be necessary to pass it.

Negro leaders decided not to support the issue unless the school were to be opened on an integrated basis. While this had not been originally planned, Negro support was perceived as so crucial to the success of the bond issue that the concession was made. If the bond issue passed, the center would be opened on an integrated basis. Election figures show that the Negro vote was indeed important. The bond passed by 1,270 votes while four Negro precincts favored it by 1,358

[38] *Ibid.*, p. 633.

to 45, a margin of 1,313. This is a clear case of bargaining and of concrete gains resulting from Negro voting strength.

Durham Negroes have not been strikingly successful otherwise in using bond issues elections to influence school policy. The DCNA supported bond issue or taxes relating to schools in 1947, 1948 and 1952, all of which passed, but would have passed even with the opposition of the Negro precincts. In 1958, when the industrial education center passed with a margin provided by Negro votes, they opposed a county school tax which would have lost even with their support.

They opposed two county school bond issues in 1960 and 1964 on grounds that they would preserve discrimination and segregation, but both issues won in spite of Negro opposition. Nevertheless, we must recognize that although their vote has not been directly influential on the outcome of many of these elections, the fact that it will be in any close election will probably encourage a more equitable distribution of bond issue funds in the future if it has not done so already.

HOSPITALS. While the Negro vote has been relevant to hospital policy in both cities, its influence has been somewhat less direct than it has in other areas. There are three hospitals in Tuskegee: a Veterans' Administration Hospital, a Tuskegee Institute Hospital and a City-County Hospital. Because the local elected bodies play no direct role in the administration of the first two, I will ignore them. The new city administration elected with Negro votes did not take initiatives in hospital policy such as they took in other areas I have investigated, partly because they shared supervisory responsibility with the County Board of Revenue. Their involvement was precipitated by a crisis.

In late summer 1965, the City-County Hospital's only doctor resigned and moved away. When the segregationist hospital board could find no white doctor to replace him, they chose to close the hospital rather than hire a Negro doctor. City and county officials met with the hospital board to try to dissuade it from closing. When they got nowhere, they requested that the board resign. Ultimately the board did resign, an integrated board was appointed, a new (white) doctor came and set up an integrated medical staff, and the hospital facilities themselves were integrated. The Negro vote was influential here, in that the hospital board probably would have closed the hospital to avoid integration were it not for the initiatives of the Negro elected Keever administration.

Durham has four general hospitals, including a Veterans' Administration Hospital and Duke University Hospital, which I will ignore as being formally removed from the influence of the vote on the local level. Although the county formally owns both Watts (predominantly white) and Lincoln Hospitals (predominantly Negro), they are both leased for twenty-five dollars or less a year to self perpetuating governing boards, which operate them essentially as private hospitals.

While Lincoln has never turned away patients because of race, it has for practical purposes been a Negro hospital since it was founded in 1901 by the Duke family "with grateful appreciation and loving remembrance of the fidelity and faithfulness of the Negro slaves to the mothers and daughters of the Confederacy during the Civil War."[39] Watts Hospital, on the other hand, was segregated up until October, 1964, when the board, after studying the prospect of integration for over a year, decided it was inevitable. The votes of Durham Negroes had nothing to do with this decision. Insofar as governmental pressure was involved, it was more directly connected with the strings on the use of federal funds for such things as hospital construction, crippled children, vocational rehabilitation, and premature births, and in anticipation of the passage of medical care for the aged under social security.

More recently, in November 1966, Durham Negroes voted against a hospital bond issue that was to give Watts Hospital $13.9 million and Lincoln $1.12 million. The Lincoln trustees had asked $3.5 million for modernization and improvement. The bond issue would have lost even with Negro support, but this is another example of how Durham's Negro voters will respond to racial dimensions of bond issue votes.

WELFARE. Both Durham and Macon Counties have local public welfare offices and local welfare boards, but both are really state, rather than local agencies. While the boards are locally appointed, they play an advisory rather than a policy-making role. The most important policy making agency in both instances is the state public welfare office and the state legislature. Except perhaps on the state level, there is no important channel through which Negro voting might influence these agencies, and there is no evidence that Negro votes have been important in the history of either agency.

UNEMPLOYMENT COMPENSATION. The Durham office of the state Employment Security Commission is even farther removed from the influence of Negro votes, at least on the local level, in that it does not even have a locally chosen advisory or governing board. It is entirely responsible to the state and federal governments, and is governed by regulations from both these sources. In Tuskegee, employment security matters are also handled by a state agency which does not have a local governing board. This agency does not even have an office in Macon County, the nearest one being in nearby Opelika.

PUBLIC HOUSING. Durham and Tuskegee both have public hous-

[39] Plaque at entrance to Lincoln Hospital.

ing projects that were formerly segregated and are now integrated. Negro voting on the local level cannot be credited in either case with securing the integration although each city government appoints a housing authority. The move can be much more directly attributed to federal policy pursuant to President Kennedy's famous "stroke of the pen" executive order of November 1962. While the locally appointed housing authorities have more impact over public housing policy than the local welfare boards have on welfare policy, they are a step removed from the direct influence of Negro votes. Recent events in Durham point up one possible channel of influence on housing policy for Negro votes. Several complaints against the housing authority, among others, were behind the recent Negro marches on city hall.[40] One of the responses of the city council, which does not directly control public housing policy, was to set up and act as a clearing house for meetings between UOCI[41] and various public agencies. One of the agencies to meet with UOCI is the housing authority. While the outcome remains uncertain, the city council, which is selected with the help of Negro votes, can help meet some Negro grievances that it cannot resolve directly by using its good offices to bring Negro leaders together with those who can.

URBAN RENEWAL. While urban renewal is not past the talking stage in Tuskegee, Durham has made plans for several projects and has begun work on a few. Two Negro census tracts, the most blighted of all the city's tracts, were entirely included in the first urban renewal project to be begun. In spite of assertions that urban renewal is equivalent to ' Negro removal, ' it must also be seen as one potential way to eliminate ghettoe and to improve life for some Negroes. Although its ultimate effect on Durham Negroes is not clear as yet, Negro voting can be very closely linked to the decision to adopt urban renewal in Durham.

Bond issue elections were again the mechanism. While the city council and most organized groups in Durham openly favored this urban renewal project, the ultimate decision to go through with it was in the hands of the electorate in the form of a bond election held in October, 1962. There were four specific bond issue questions which involved the city's share of the cost of the project. Each of these four questions passed by narrow margins, an average of 237 votes out of over 9,500. The four Negro precincts contributed an average balance of 1,807 votes in favor of the four questions. Quite clearly, urban renewal would have lost if Negroes had not turned out, if they had split, or if they had voted in the opposite direction. This is one of those relatively

[40] See above, p. 56-57.
[41] United Organizations for Community Improvement, the spearhead of the demands.

rare cases in which a major possibility for concrete advantages for Negroes can be clearly and directly attributed to Negro voting strength.

APPOINTMENTS TO BOARDS, COMMISSIONS AND CIVIL SERVICE JOBS

Patronage in the form of public jobs and honorific appointments is one of the oldest forms of rewards for group voting in American politics. At least since the time of Andrew Jackson it has been common for elected officials to reward their supporters with the economic security of a public job or with the prestige of an appoinment to an official board. Myrdal says that "it has become customary to distribute jobs . . . in some relation to the voting strength of the various regional, national and religious groups in the community,"[42] and, in fact, this is one of the first gains many Negro political leaders have sought. While changing styles of politics are changing the basis for determining who shall be in the public employ, public employment is one of the places where Negro votes may bring rewards.

APPOINTMENT TO POSITIONS ON BOARDS AND COMMISSIONS is not only an honor, but also a means of access to centers of policy formation. In Tuskegee, there was an abrupt change from no Negroes on boards and commissions before the watershed year of 1964, to very extensive Negro appointments since then. Negroes now sit in 12 of the 21 seats on the city's biracial committee. They hold two of five positions on the city library board, three of five on the housing authority, three of seven on the city planning board, one of three on the medical-clinical board, five of nine on the recreation board, two of seven on the board of pensions and welfare, and four of ten on the board of directors of the city-county hospital. There is no appointive board in Tuskegee without direct Negro representation.

The city of Durham has fifteen official boards and commissions, and Negroes are now on nine of them. These appointments have taken place over a long period of time. The first board to have Negroes on it was the Stanford L. Warren Library board, which has always been entirely Negro, as the library's clientele has been virtually all Negro. A Negro was appointed to the city recreation commission in 1944 when it was first established. This was the first time a Negro had been appointed to a predominantly white city board in Durham. In 1949 a Negro was appointed to the newly created housing authority. The board of education, which is appointed by the city council in Durham, was naturally

[42] *Op. cit.*, p. 435.

one of the bodies on which Negroes were most eager to have representation. In 1951 the Negroes asked that John H. Wheeler, then as now one of the most prominent Negro citizens, be appointed, but he was considered objectionable because of the role he had played in the recent litigation against the board. The council offered the appointment instead to C. C. Spaulding, president of the North Carolina Mutual Life Insurance Company, a founder of the DCNA, and perhaps the most prominent Durham Negro at that time. Spaulding declined reportedly because he felt, as did other Negro leaders, that Negroes ought to be able to choose their own representative to the board. The council may have offered him the position knowing that he would not accept. Whether this is the case or not is not clear, but in any event, no Negro was appointed to the board until 1958, seven years later.

Negroes were first appointed to the board of adjustment in 1955, to the "biracial" Human Relations Committee when it was first created in 1957, to the urban renewal commission in 1958, to the planning and zoning commission in 1961, and to the "Good Neighbor Council" when it was created in 1963. Four of the six commissions which do not have Negro representation are technical boards for which there are professional qualifications. They are the board of electrical examiners, heating contractor's examining board, plumber's board of examiners and the subdivision control board. The other two include the airport authority and the public library board. When the two libraries have completed the process of merger, there will be one integrated board.

While the link between votes and appointments is much clearer in Tuskegee than in Durham, there is reason to believe that there is such a link in both cases. In Tuskegee, the process is quite uncomplicated. The old city council never saw fit to appoint any Negro to any board or commission. It was replaced with a council elected by a Negro majority, which was more than willing to appoint qualified Negroes to these posts. In Durham, the process was slower and more piecemeal, but the process covaried with the growth of Negro voting, and Negro leaders let it be known that they were interested in such rewards for their voting support. There is no evidence that would lead to the rejection of a hypothesis that the gains were at least in part causally related to Negro votes.

PUBLIC EMPLOYMENT. In Tuskegee, the *ancien régime* was not unwilling to hire Negroes to city employment; it was merely unwilling to hire them to any but menial jobs. About half of the city's work force was Negro before 1964, but they all worked in the streets, sanitation and light departments, which needed a substantial labor force. After Negro votes replaced that regime with a new council, the new administration hired eleven Negroes to positions that had been formerly closed to them. These positions included a clerk working in the front office of city hall, one of the two full-time firemen, five patrolmen, two sergeants and an operator in a police department with a staff of eighteen, and a water and filtering plant operator. Now 63.3 percent of city employment is Negro. The role of Negro votes in effecting the changes is obvious.

A clear analysis of the Durham situation is more elusive.[43] The same changes that have taken place so abruptly in Tuskegee have been taking place in Durham slowly over a period of more than twenty years, and less obviously as a result of Negro voting. For example, Negro police were first hired in Durham in 1944, probably at least in part in response to organized Negro requests of city hall. Yet however important political influence was, it was probably not the only factor. White policemen are believed to be less effective in Negro neighborhoods because of their reluctance to patrol there and because they may be less effective in dealing with Negro offenders. The city officials who made the decision to hire Negro police were no doubt aware of this, perhaps because the Negro leaders had made their case in those terms. By 1951, two Negroes had been promoted to detective status and one to lieutenant. In 1964 two more Negroes were promoted to detective. A Negro was recently assigned to downtown traffic duty for the first time. The first Negro firemen were hired in 1958 to man the newly completed fire station in the main Negro district. This gain, along with the fire station itself, was a result of a concession in a bond issue election.[44]

For some time Negroes have filled positions as recreation division director and as treatment plant supervisors. Within the past five or so years, Negroes have been hired as meter readers and as drivers of sanitation trucks, positions previously filled by whites only. A Negro was recently promoted to foreman of a buildings and grounds crew for the first time, and the first Negro housing inspector was hired a few years ago.

For years, Durham Negroes have been complaining that there has been no Negro clerical help in city hall, and in 1965 a Negro woman was hired as a bookkeeper in the city payroll office, and in 1967 another was placed in the water billing department. Negroes have been hired as cashiers in the new municipal parking garage. Perhaps most remarkable is that a white man has been hired to a position under supervision of a Negro. To what extent can this series of firsts be credited to Negro voting?

---

[43] See Keech, *op. cit.*, pp. 159-72 for further details on Durham.
[44] See above, pp. 63-64.

If it is a result of Negro voting, it is clearly not the result of a sharp change in regime as was the case in Tuskegee. Insofar as the 'regime' has changed in Durham with regard to racial matters, it has done so very slowly and in a piecemeal fashion. DCNA leaders have for years been asking the city to hire Negroes to positions that were formerly closed to them, and one way to account for the changes would be to argue that candidates responded to these demands because they were supported by votes. I see no reason to reject this hypothesis, although for the most part both DCNA leaders and city councilmen deplore the very implication that they trade favors for votes. I suspect that they overstate the case somewhat, but the fact remains that most Durham public officials prefer to view themselves as impartial arbiters of the public weal rather than as bargainers who trade votes for 'favors.'

Another hypothesis can help account for the increasing number of Negroes in positions that were formerly closed to them. Negro votes may have helped elect candidates who were more 'fair-minded' than their opponents, in the sense that they were more willing to hire the most qualified candidate for any job regardless of color. If past officials had been more fair-minded, they might have seen to it that jobs were not closed to Negroes simply because they were Negro. By helping replace such incumbents with men who would support open competition for all positions, Negro votes could have contributed to opening up more of public employment to Negroes. In either case, I see no evidence to reject the hypothesis that Negro votes helped bring about more job opportunities in Durham's city government as well as Tuskegee's.

THE EFFECT OF NEGRO VOTES IN THE PUBLIC SECTOR

In Tuskegee, Negro votes have had a clear and direct effect on who is elected to public office, on street paving and garbage collection in Negro areas, on recreation, library and hospital facilities available to Negroes, and on who is chosen to appointive boards and civil service positions. Negro votes are relevant to treatment by police and courts, fire protection, schools and public housing, even though they have not as yet played a demonstrably important role in these policies. Votes have been for the most part irrelevant to welfare and unemployment policy.

In Durham, Negro votes have had a demonstrable impact on who is elected to public office, on the distribution of fire stations and recreation facilities and on the decision to have urban renewal. Votes have been relevant and probably important in treatment of Negroes by police and courts, and in effecting appointment of Negroes to boards and commissions and civil service positions. Negro votes have been irrelevant in street paving, welfare and unemployment policy. In other areas of the public sector in Durham, the role of the vote has been quite problematic.

CHAPTER V

The Payoffs of Negro Voting: The Private Sector and the Effects of Past Discrimination

AT THIS POINT all of the discussion of payoffs to Negroes has been about the public sector, that portion of social life which is directly controlled or administered by government, with special emphasis on activity on the local government level. But even in an era of expanding scope of government and a growing public sector, the bulk of social life still takes place outside the direct control of government. At least until recently, public accommodations, employment and the sale and rental of housing have been left relatively unaffected by governments, yet practices in these areas, particularly the last two, have crucially important bearing on the status and opportunities of Negroes. Further, eliminating discrimination in the present is not going to put Negroes on an equal footing with whites, but rather decades of past discrimination will leave their mark even after most forms of current day discrimination are eliminated. Consequently it becomes important to investigate the impact of the vote on the private sector and the effects of past discrimination as well as its impact on the public sector.

PAYOFFS IN THE PRIVATE SECTOR

Discrimination in employment has been one of the major contributors to the subordinate social and economic status of Negroes. For years they have been considered only for low level jobs which are for Negroes only, and for as many years they have been denied employment in favor of comparably or less qualified whites. This has perhaps been the major obstacle to upward mobility and the fulfillment of the American dream for the Negro. Similarly the existence of different housing markets for whites and Negroes has made it very difficult, if not impossible, for many Negroes to buy or rent homes in keeping with their tastes and resources. It has confined most Negroes to slum housing in ghettos which expand only with the flight of whites from substandard housing on the fringes. It has allowed landlords to charge higher rents than their dwellings would bring in a completely open market. Also, Negroes have been denied equal access to restaurants, places of entertainment, hotels and motels, etc. All such discrimination has contributed to a vicious circle of poverty and ghetto living which feeds on itself.

If the vote is to be very useful in eliminating injustice against Negroes and putting them on an equal footing with other Americans, it will have to do something in these areas. To what extent, then, has the vote in Durham and Tuskegee helped Negroes there to secure fair treatment in the private sector of social life?

When the first "Negro-elected" city council took office in Tuskegee in 1964, the Federal Civil Rights Act of that year had already been passed, so there was already some legislation dealing with public accommodations and fair employment in Tuskegee when this first council which was responsive to Negro demands was elected. However, the two restaurants affected by the public accommodations provision reconstituted themselves as private clubs, and only one firm had enough employees to be subject to the fair employment provision. Thus supplementary legislation became necessary.

The Tuskegee city council did act on the matter, but not until 1966. The first action was a public accommodations ordinance passed in January to supplement the federal law, but the real payoff came in October of that year, when far-reaching fair employment and public accommodations ordinances were passed. The fair employment ordinance prohibits discrimination in connection with "hiring, application for employment, tenure, promotion, upgrading, increasing in compensation, terms or conditions of employment," and it applies to employers of two or more persons. Violators are subject to fines up to one hundred dollars, and imprisonment up to ninety days, or both. Persons violating the act two or more times within a twelve month period will have their license revoked for at least six months.

The public accommodations ordinance guarantees full and equal use of all facilities and privileges of "any place of public accommodation, resort or amusement" in Tuskegee or its police jurisdiction. It applies to facilities ranging from hotels, motels, restaurants and theaters to ice cream parlors, bath-houses, hospitals, circuses, billiard parlors, shooting galleries, public conveyances operated on land, water and air, and even elevators of buildings operated by more than one tenant. Violators are subject to the same punishments as in the fair employment ordinance.[1]

Accounting for these ordinances would be very difficult without the Negro vote. Few facts are more certain than that the *ancien régime* city council in Tuskegee would not have passed such ordinances willingly. The process is perfectly unambiguous. The new Negro majority replaced the old council with a new one of their own choosing, with which they felt they could work. The new council passed the ordinances in question.

Some local observers have noted that the first public accommodations ordinance was not passed until soon after demonstrations that followed the murder of a young Negro by a white man. Negro demands were stepped up somewhat at that time, but even if the murder and the demonstrations were catalytic, it does not follow that the vote was not at the root of the willingness of the council to pass such an ordinance. There was dilatory behavior on the part of at least one city official which postponed the ultimate appearance of the final two ordinances, but it was not by an elective member of the city administration. The important point is that the acts were passed, and that they would not have been were it not for the ability of the Negro vote to replace the old administration with one that was responsive to such demands.

There have been striking changes in Durham as well in opening up employment opportunities and public accommodations to Negroes, but the Negro vote was far less useful there than it was in Tuskegee. Most indicative of this is the fact that the changes in the private sector took place without the direct or official involvement of the city council. Durham Negroes used other political resources and techniques much more effectively than the vote in this case. Direct pressure in the form of demonstration, sit-in and boycott were much more instrumental in securing changes than was the Negro vote.

Evidence on the role of the vote in opening up public accommodations and jobs to Negroes in Durham is based on an analysis of how the decisions to improve the lot of Negroes in the private sector were made. While there is a kind of crude covariation between the growth of Negro voting and the opening of public accommodations, etc., this is a spurious relationship. Many changes were made as a result of identifiable decisions in which it will be obvious that the vote played a minor role at best. The city council, where we would expect the vote to be influential, was not helpful in eliminating private dis-

[1] *The Tuskegee News,* October 27, 1966.

crimination. Indeed, we can begin by showing a few cases where the city council passed up an opportunity to be helpful.

For example, the city owns the ballpark used by the local minor league baseball team and one of the local movie theaters, both of which are leased to private enterprise. Because of this, the city is in a good position to influence the racial policies of both establishments through the lease. Certainly a city council committed to racial equality would have done so, but Durham continued to pass up opportunities to demand integration by the lessees, even when the leases expired. Thus Negroes trying to integrate these public accommodations were left on the same footing as with the privately owned facilities.

Interestingly, one rationale for the city council's policy was the obverse of that which led to integration of parks and library. In those cases, the city attorney had advised that the city had no legal basis for maintaining segregation, and that it would lose any lawsuits to integrate. In the case of the city owned theater, the attorney advised just the reverse. He pointed out that the theater's desegregation policy was private action and that by amending the unexpired lease to demand integration the city could be subject to costly litigation which it might lose and, thereby, to extensive damages. The council took his advice, which suggests that in integration of both city operated and city leased facilities the prospects of litigation influenced the city more than Negro votes did.

Even when the leases were up for renewal, only the Negro councilman ever dissented from votes to renew them on the same basis. At one point in 1958 even the Negro councilman voted with the unanimous council to extend one of the leases on the previous basis. Whether he was caught napping on the integration issue or was simply unconcerned, this does not speak well of his efforts in behalf of the Negro community. He was, however, a lone dissenter on second reading.

While it came close, the city did fall short of absolutely no effort to integrate the facilities it leased. In 1962, when the theater was being picketed and the city appointed Human Relations Committee was trying to get the city to act, the council refused to *request* that its lessee desegregate. The motion of the Negro councilman to that effect failed for lack of second. Later the council did go on record unanimously as being "unopposed to integration," and requested that the manager meet with those who are seeking integration and with the Human Relations Committee to try to negotiate a solution. This is significant in that it marked the farthest that the city had gone by 1962 toward openly endorsing integration anywhere.

The first serious attempt to integrate any privately owned public accommodations in Durham occurred in June, 1957, almost three years before the national sit-in movement began in Greensboro. It involved a militant young Negro minister and six companions sitting down and asking for service on the white side of a dairy bar. The group refused to leave when asked by the manager to do so, and were subsequently convicted of trespassing and fined, later losing an appeal that went all the way to the United States Supreme Court. While losing in the courts, the Negroes kept up a boycott of the dairy bar for six years, including pickets at times, and ultimately prevailed. In March of 1963, all seats were removed and separate entrances were done away with.

General boycotts of business establishments discriminating against Negroes in hiring practices took place in 1961 and 1963 with some success. Some Durham Negroes argue that the threat of a bus boycott was important in leading the Duke Power Company to hire Negroes to drive the city's busses. There is no reason to believe that the Negro vote played any role in opening up these job opportunities.

One week after the national sit-in movement started in Greensboro in February 1960, sit-ins were initiated in Durham.[2] The following events are important to our analysis mainly because of how they demonstrate the reluctance of the Durham city council to become involved. Very soon after the sit-ins began, the mayor asked the city council-appointed Human Relations Committee (HRC) to negotiate the dispute, and this committee did work to bring about a settlement that would involve the integration of the lunch counters. This, however, was the closest the council came to direct involvement. Indeed, the council passed up a few opportunities to play a constructive role.

Because the national policy of the stores was to operate according to 'local customs,' the chairman of the Human Relations Committee realized that one way to approach the problem might be to ask store managers, demonstration leaders and the city council what they would "recognize as a true expression of the voice of the total community." None of them, including the city council, so much as responded.

The HRC, which had developed a 'three point proposal' to resolve the dispute, had agreed to seek specific guidance from the city council about how to proceed from the impasse they had reached. When they sought such guidance, the press erroneously reported that the HRC had asked the council to adopt its 'three point proposal,' rather than for guidance. The council apparently did not want to involve itself at all, and concentrating on this misreporting of facts, asked the city attorney

[2] The following account of the 1960 sit-ins and the 1963 demonstrations depends heavily on Allan P. Sindler, "Negro Protest and Local Politics in Durham, N. C." (Eagleton Institute Cases in Practical Politics, No. 37, 1965).

whether they had the legal power to adopt the proposal. The attorney told them that they lacked the power to enforce the proposal if adopted, and the council then dropped the entire matter.

By August, seven months after the sit-ins had begun, the store managers responded to the sit-ins, a boycott, the efforts of the HRC and the apparent success of the movement in other cities, and integrated the lunch counters. The very use of demonstrations to secure integration says something about the unimportance of the vote. Insofar as the Durham Negro vote was effective and relevant at all, it was through its role in selecting a mayor and council that would appoint a conciliatory biracial committee like the Human Relations Committee, and in selecting a mayor that would use it. Still, other than giving the ball to the HRC, the council, many of whose members were elected with the help of Negro votes, could hardly have done less than it did to secure integration of the lunch counters.

The vote played a more crucial, although still a secondary role in the most important single series of events in opening up public accommodations and fair employment opportunities to Durham Negroes. The major impetus for the changes seems to have been mass demonstrations in early 1963 which were initiated by the NAACP chapter at North Carolina College, the local state institution for Negroes. The college NAACP leaders decided to capitalize on the groundswell of concern created by the racial violence in Birmingham, Alabama, and particularly the use of police dogs and fire hoses there.

The demonstrations began on the day city council elections were held in May of 1963, and continued for two days afterwards, drawing more and more people each time. Approximately 1,400 were arrested and it appeared to numerous observers that Durham was on the brink of the sort of racial violence that had brought infamy to several other southern cities. The demonstrations were not the only important events on that election day, however. The election of a new mayor was to be important in determining the outcome of the demonstrations themselves.

This new mayor, R. Wensell Grabarek, responded to this delicate and potentially violent situation with skill and finesse. His leadership, plus the fear of others in the community that violence would make Durham another Birmingham helped to bring about a settlement favorable to Negro interests. Grabarek initiated a series of meetings with the demonstration leaders wherein he asked them to consolidate their requests and promised to deal with them without equivocation. These meetings also resulted in the temporary and conditional cessation of demonstrations, providing an atmosphere more conducive to the negotiation and persuasion that was ultimately to achieve so much.

The principal demands of the student leaders were for fair employment practices and public accommodations ordinances, but the response to them was in terms of voluntary change rather than legal enactment. This was apparently at Grabarek's initiative. Rather than taking the requests to the city council for consideration, he met with about sixty business and civic leaders and confronted them with the civil rights problem the city was then facing. After this meeting it was decided that Grabarek should appoint a committee

to review the entire breadth and scope of civil rights matters with the aim to resolve or reconcile all matters of racial differences existing among the people of our community . . . (with) specific instructions . . . to seek the highest possible level of understanding, on a totally voluntary basis, acceptable to all parties directly concerned.[3]

The job of this committee was to seek voluntary changes that would come as close as possible to being the functional equivalent of the two requested ordinances without confronting the issues of legal enactment. Probably, this was viewed as the most likely method of securing the desired changes without splitting the community and without leading to the defeat of attempts to secure the changes. It was an attempt to meet the demands of the Negroes for integration of public accommodations and opening of fair employment opportunities without forcing compliance and without providing the risk for elected public officials that compulsory legal enactment would have.

In the following weeks the Durham Interim Committee (DIC) worked with the full support of the mayor to persuade businessmen to alter their discriminatory practices. They emphasized the inevitability of changes in racial patterns and described the alternatives as making voluntary adjustments on the one hand or giving in after a long, bitter struggle that would be destructive of the community's welfare on the other.

In its final report, submitted to the mayor July 12, 1963, the DIC related that forty-one retail merchants with over 1,300 employees had pledged themselves to hire on the basis of qualification and without regard to race, creed, color or national origin. Three insurance companies with local home offices and six commercial banks indicated that their hiring practices would be based solely on the qualifications of the applicant and not at all on race. Duke University advised that its policy for some time had been to hire without regard to race. Several industries under contract with the federal government had been operating under fair employment practices required by Washington for some time.

[3] Durham Interim Committee Report, June 4, 1963, pp. 3-4.

All told, the firms identifying themselves as adhering to fair employment practices which were covered by this report represented over 13,900 employees, out of the work force of a city of almost 80,000.[4]

Of course, such voluntary affirmation is not the functional equivalent of an enforceable ordinance, because no-one is forced to agree, and because those who do may talk more effective fair employment than they practice. Without procedures for handling complaints and some effective means of securing compliance, there is no guarantee that those who promise fair employment will practice it. How many Negroes were actually hired as a result of the DIC's efforts is not known.

The city's leading hotel desegregated, but the other declined. All eleven of the motels had desegregated. Food service establishments "representing more than 90 percent of the Durham food volume" and including "all of the major restaurants, cafeterias, cafes, and grills" had agreed to serve the public without regard to race or color.[5]

Integration of the movie theaters had not been achieved by the time of the committee's final report, but by the fall only one of the city's indoor theaters remained segregated. Here again, of course, voluntary affirmation is not equivalent to enforceable law, although the difference may be less serious than in the case of fair employment. A subcommittee did file a brief with the city attorney on the question of whether or not the city had been granted the power to pass such a law by the state legislature, but nothing ever came of it.

On the suggestion of the Interim Committee, the city council resolved that "discrimination because of race, creed, color or national origin is contrary to the constitutional principles and policies of the United States, of the State of North Carolina and of the City and County of Durham,"[6] and empowered the mayor to set up a permanent committee to succeed it, which he did in April of 1964. The only other official act of the council on these matters was to repeal an ordinance *requiring* segregation of the races in restaurants—after a number of restaurant owners had agreed to integrate, and two years after the city attorney had advised the council that it was null and void for constitutional reasons.

To what extent can we account for these changes with Negro voting strength in Durham? The most immediate causes were the demonstrations with the accompanying threat of violence, the perception of many leaders that change was inevitable, and the hard work of the mayor and the Interim Committee in securing the cooperation and

[4] Durham Interim Committee Report, July 12, 1963, p. 4.
[5] *Ibid.,* p. 10.
[6] Durham City Council Minute Book DD, p. 65.

compliance of Durham business establishments. It is unlikely that the businesses that went along with the urging of the Interim Committee would have done so without the strong urging of their peers and leaders on the Committee that change was inevitable, and that failure to concede now would mean the possibility of violence and long bitter conflict that would only delay and not deter change. It is also unlikely that these leaders would have been mobilized without the initial stimulus, indeed threat of the demonstrations.[7]

All of these factors are independent of Negro voting strength, and one of the clearest features of the entire episode is that the city council, which should be most responsive to Negro voting strength, did about as little as it possibly could have short of actively obstructing change. Their inactivity is a clear indication of some of the limitations of voting strength in this area.

The role of the vote appears more significant, however, when we look at the activity of the newly elected mayor. Overestimating the importance of his immediate and straightforward response to Negro demands and his staking of his prestige on the Interim Committee would be hard. There is no doubt that his persuasiveness helped to effect many of the gains that were made, and there is no doubt that the Negro vote was important in electing him. His opponent led in the white and mixed precincts by 279 votes, but with the four Negro precincts included in the totals, Grabarek won by 2,245 votes. Grabarek received 89.2 percent of the votes in the Negro precincts.

One wonders what would have happened if his opponent had been elected. Although Grabarek had been endorsed by the DCNA, the differences between him and his opponent were not striking. Sindler says that "there was little in Grabarek's record which would have led one to predict the quality of leadership and the sensitivity to the race issue which he subsequently exhibited as mayor."[8] Still, his opponent must be given a great deal of the credit for the gains that were made, as he was chairman of the Interim Committee. Perhaps the fact that two such men were the candidates is itself partly a result of the Negro vote. Even

---

[7] For a literary account which illustrates some of the limits as well as possibilities of demonstrations in opening public accommodations, see John Ehle, *The Free Men* (New York: Harper and Row, 1965), a treatment of civil rights activity in Chapel Hill, N. C.

[8] Sindler, *op. cit.,* p. 15. Grabarek, however, is no longer at all heroic to the Durham Negro community. After it became known that the DCNA would endorse his opponent in 1967, he campaigned with the slogan "I will not get the 'bloc' vote." Also, there have been some heated exchanges between him and Negroes petitioning the city council.

so the overall impact of Negro votes on the opening up of the private sector remains very limited.

Federal public accommodations and fair employment legislation as well as the local legislation on these matters in Tuskegee have rendered them for the most part dead issues in both cities. But this does not mean that, even insofar as discrimination in public accommodations and employment has been eliminated there, all private sector discrimination has been eliminated. Racial discrimination in the sale and rental of housing has scarcely become an important public issue in either city. This is not to say that it is not a problem. While Durham has a far worse ghetto problem than Tuskegee, it would not have been possible for Tuskegee's old city council to gerrymander virtually all of the Negroes out of the city limits if there had not been rather extreme residential segregation there. The closest Negroes have come to demanding action on this matter in Durham is to demand that the city build more public housing units in places other than the main Negro ghetto. At this point nothing has happened in either city to eliminate racial segregation in housing. This lack of action leaves matters clear and simple for our analysis of the role of the vote. Even the present high level of Negro voting in either city has done nothing about this problem.

THE EFFECTS OF PAST DISCRIMINATION

The types of discrimination I have matched against the influence of the Negro vote were meant to include some reflection of all forms of current discrimination we can expect to be subject to political action. Thus I have not investigated the influence of votes on interpersonal discrimination in the choice of friends and associates, for example, because there is no apparent way of securing such a policy through governmental action, and because few would seek such a measure anyway.

Still, we cannot conclude that these investigations have covered all the ways in which government action might be expected to remedy discrimination against Negroes. If it were the case that in some setting all of the forms of discrimination we have studied were completely eliminated, we would still not quickly find Negroes on an equal footing with whites. The disparity would remain, for example, in schools where long years of deprivation would still leave their mark. It would remain in employment, where even under standards of scrupulous fairness in hiring, Negroes can expect to be hired less often than whites. It would be winking at injustice to say that other things being equal, the Negro would have an equal chance. *Other things will not be equal even when all current discrimination is eliminated.* Today's Negro bears the marks of decades of discrimination and deprivation which cannot be wiped out overnight.

As Charles Silberman puts it,

The American Negro has been subject to a system designed to destroy ambition, prevent independence, and erode intelligence for the past three and a half centuries.[9]

If all discrimination were to end immediately, that alone would not materially improve the Negro's position.[10]

St. Clair Drake asks whether the victimization resulting from unequal treatment of Negroes in the past can be eliminated without preferential treatment for present day victims.[11] As Thomas Pettigrew states the problem, it is not merely one of "allowing Negroes to enter the mainstream of American life but of *enabling* them to enter."[12]

The problem is *how* to enable Negroes to enter the mainstream, and a growing number of suggestions has been proposed. For example, Pettigrew has proposed some structural reforms which include broadened minimum wage legislation, exemption of the poor from income taxes and crash programs of job training and retraining.[13] Martin Luther King suggested a guaranteed income.[14] James Tobin concludes that "the single most important step the nation could take to improve the economic position of the Negro is to operate the economy steadily at a low rate of unemployment."[15] The programs of the Federal government's war on poverty represent a good many of the suggestions that have been made, although it remains to be seen how successful they will be.[16]

[9] Charles E. Silberman, *Crisis in Black and White* (New York: Random House, 1964), p. 77.
[10] *Ibid.*, p. 70.
[11] "The Social and Economic Status of the Negro in the United States," in Talcott Parsons and Kenneth B. Clark, eds., *The Negro American* (Boston: Beacon Press, 1967), p. 39.
[12] Thomas F. Pettigrew, *A Profile of the Negro American* (Princeton, N. J.: D. Van Nostrand Co., Inc., 1964), p. 161.
[13] *Ibid.*, pp. 168-77.
[14] *New York Times Magazine,* June 11, 1967, p. 102.
[15] "On Improving the Economic Status of the Negro," in Parsons and Clark, *op. cit.,* p. 457. For some striking data on the relationship between the unemployment rate for nonwhite males and cases opened under AFDC, and that between nonwhite male unemployment and the percent of nonwhite married women separated from their husbands, see Daniel Patrick Moynihan, "Employment, Income and the Negro Family" in Parsons and Clark, *op. cit.,* pp. 154, 157.
[16] See Silberman, *op. cit., passim,* and Pettigrew, *op. cit.,* pp. 159-68, 177 for arguments that part of the Negro's problems is personal and somewhat independent of structural reforms like those mentioned above.

The point here, however, is not to discuss the relative merits of the various programs and proposals. Rather, the prospects that Negro political influence, and specifically Negro votes, will help to resolve these more long range problems of the Negro will be discussed. The experiences of Durham and Tuskegee do not lead to encouraging conclusions.

As one of Tuskegee's Negro citizens put it, the admittedly remarkable advances that have been made in that city are the "obvious" ones, but not the "fundamental" changes that are necessary. According to him, Negro leaders in Tuskegee are too cautious. They set their sights too low and are too conservative in their estimates of what can be done and in terms of what whites will accept. In Durham, the same complaint has been raised many times, but in Durham, the more dynamic Negro organizations like neighborhood councils are still working on some of the "obvious" advances, like housing code enforcement, and with less than complete success.

The Durham and Tuskegee Negro organizations that have been so successful in mobilizing a Negro electorate and in securing important concessions through the courts are no longer at the forefront of the "Negro revolution." These organizations are led by middle class business and professional people who no longer suffer in any marked degree from either present discrimination or the effects of past discrimination. They are persons who have broken out of the cycle of poverty (if all of them were in it). They are already *in* the "mainstream of American life." That they are not highly vocal in emphasizing problems that they do not suffer from, and in suggesting solutions to them, is not surprising.

But even if it is true that the DCNA and the MCDC are not directly involved in the problems of the ghetto; it is not apparent that they could use the vote very effectively to solve those problems on the local level. The suggestions for enabling Negroes to enter the mainstream of American life cited above are for the most part programs that demand Federal action. Local governments have limited tools and financial resources with which to attack these problems, though Negro votes for Federal government officials can and probably have contributed to their adoption. Perhaps the most the local vote can be expected to do is to help elect national officials who will support such programs, and to help elect local officials who will cooperate with the Federal programs. Lest there be undue optimism on this, at one point the U. S. Department of Labor ruled Durham schools ineligible for a Neighborhood Youth Corps project because the city school board had not yet complied with the 1964 Civil Rights Act.[17] At another the Durham school board chose not to

[17] *Durham Morning Herald,* November 10, 1965.

participate in Project Headstart because of changes which were requested in its application, one of which was a statement of compliance with the 1964 Civil Rights Act.[18] On still a third occasion the board turned down a Neighborhood Youth Corps program. One of the board members' arguments against it was that "I don't think the school board should get into a welfare program."[19]

But the problem is not so much that the leaders of established Negro political organizations are not very aggressive or resourceful in trying to eliminate the effects of past discrimination, that the Federal government has not developed some programs designed to attack and break the cycle of poverty, or that Negro votes do not always move local officials to participate in such programs when they are available. The real problem is more serious. It is that nobody really knows how to eliminate the effects of America's history of discrimination against Negroes. The problems are not the kind that can be resolved by simply enlisting the good will of all persons concerned, or by securing concessions from important power groups defending the status quo. The problems of the civil rights movement (which are not entirely solved) were child's play in comparison. The basic problem of that movement was to get whites to cooperate with Negroes in treating them fairly, equally and on a par with white citizens. The problem was to end active discrimination. This provided no intellectual difficulties. Once white Americans could be moved to stop discriminating, the discrimination would stop. The problems are no longer so easy.

[18] *Ibid.*, March 30, 31, 1966.
[19] *Ibid.*, May 17, 1966. This program was later reinstated. See *ibid.*, May 25, 1966.

CHAPTER VI

Conclusions

WE ARE NOW in a position to draw together our findings and to analyze them for their significance in situations other than Durham and Tuskegee. Tuskegee yields the clearest and most easily interpreted patterns. Negro votes were obviously instrumental in securing a very extensive turnover among those who are elected to public office, including the election of many Negroes. Negro votes brought a radical change in the distribution of public services, including garbage collection, street paving and recreation facilities. Negroes were hired for the first time to municipal service positions and appointed to boards and commissions as a result of Negro votes, and those votes were also instrumental in bringing about the passage of local public accommodations and fair employment ordinances. Negro votes played a somewhat lesser role in eliminating discrimination in hospitals, and discrimination in schools and jury selection was dealt with through court suits initiated before Negro voting had reached sufficient strength to secure them. Still, it is likely that none of these things would have been beyond the influence of Negro votes in contemporary Tuskegee were they left to that process for resolution.

Clearly, then, Negro voting in Tuskegee has achieved some remarkable gains. Indeed, it has been instrumental in erasing most of the *existing* mechanisms of discrimination in that city. In this sense we could argue that the vote has secured a very important measure of justice: fair and equal treatment by government, and the legal prohibition of discrimination in employment and public accommodations, two of the most important areas of discrimination in the private sector.

But to conclude an analysis of these matters in Tuskegee at such a point would be to ignore the most poignant lessons of that city. Saying that votes bring fair treatment of Negroes in Tuskegee is different only in degree from saying votes bring fair treatment of Jews in Tel Aviv. Negroes are a majority of the electorate in Tuskegee. More important than the fact that this majority secured the specified gains is the fact that having 35, 40 and 45 percent of the electorate was not enough! Saying that the vote is a protector of majorities in a democracy means little. Cohesive and intense majorities do not as a rule need protection.

The vote failed the Negro in Tuskegee when it was most needed. All of the above mentioned gains came abruptly when the Negroes became a majority of the electorate. Before that the situation was much like any other black belt Alabama city in spite of the fact that Negroes comprised more than a third of the registered electorate for years. When Negroes were a minority of the electorate, they were left out in the cold, even though they were a very substantial minority. Tuskegee is as important as a demonstration of what votes do not bring as it is of what they can bring.

If Tuskegee demonstrates that under some conditions it takes a majority of votes to secure some basic rights, Durham exemplifies how less than a majority can secure some gains, and demonstrates some of the limits on what voting can achieve in more nearly ordinary situations. The Durham situation is more complicated than that of Tuskegee. Negro voting is not the clear, direct and unambiguous cause of anything in the sense that it is in Tuskegee. However, the vote was relevant to influence over the outcome of elections, to securing equal treatment by law enforcement agencies, to equal distribution of such public goods as parks and fire stations, to employment of Negroes in municipal service, and to appointments to boards and commissions.

In Durham, too, the failures of the vote are as significant as its success. The fact that the vote has not helped pave streets in Negro areas is at least partially due to Durham's system of having residents pay for paving of their own streets. The failure of the vote to be useful in integrating parks, schools and libraries is more significant, and more directly attributable to the limitations of the vote as a political resource for minorities. Fair employment and integration in the private sector of social life was even farther removed from the influence of the vote in Durham. The general picture there seems to be that the vote is most useful for the least important gains. Surely the greatest strides made by Durham Negroes themselves have been the integration of schools and public accommodations, and the extension of fair employment. The things the vote has most clearly helped them secure are far less dramatic than these changes.

WHERE NEGRO VOTES ARE MOST USEFUL

Even though this research has been almost entirely limited to two cities, the analysis has been sufficiently revealing to yield several hypotheses that are relevant to other situations. In this section I will develop hypotheses about which kinds of policies are most resistant or least resistant to the impact of Negro votes. These hypotheses will not reveal how many gains to expect in a given community at a given level of Negro voting strength and a given context of other conditions. Such prediction is beyond the present capabilities of virtually all areas of political science. But they will, I hope, point out what kinds of payoffs to expect first or last, and in a given situation they should be useful in identifying what gains to seek next as those most likely to yield to the influence of Negro votes.

1. The effects of past discrimination are far more resistant to Negro voting than is present discrimination. In Tuskegee, where Negro votes have done more to eliminate present discrimination than in any city I know of, the problems of eliminating the effects of past discrimination have scarcely become a public issue. Durham has not even gone so far as Tuskegee in eliminating present discrimination. Neither city has taken initiatives that go beyond having local community action and anti-poverty agencies which are supported by the Office of Economic Opportunity, and in Durham there has been important resistance to even this.[1] One of the reasons the effects of past discrimination are so resistant to the power of Negro votes is that nobody, including Negro leaders, really knows what to do about them. Still, Negro votes are expected to help make it a recognized public issue, but votes seem not to have done this in either city. A further problem is that programs which are designed to eliminate the effects of past discrimination are likely to generate considerable opposition because they appear to discriminate in *favor* of Negroes.[2] Still another part of the problem is that so many Americans, including some Negro leaders, seem not to have begun to think about the Negro problem in terms of the effects of past discrimination, although the failure of the gains of the civil rights movement to radically improve the status of American Negroes is making it more

---

[1] See above, pp. 91-92.

[2] However, the programs of the federal "war on poverty," which come as close as anything American government is doing to alleviate the effects of past discrimination, were neither designed by Negroes, nor the result of specific Negro demands, nor aimed explicitly at resolving the problems of Negroes. Were these things the case, passing the programs would probably have been much more difficult. See comments to this effect by James Q. Wilson in "The Negro in Politics," in Talcott Parsons and Kenneth B. Clark, eds., *The Negro American* (Boston: The Beacon Press, 1965), p. 434.

apparent all the time that the ' Negro problem ' is still a national crisis.

2. In attacking present discrimination against Negroes, Negro votes are less able to secure fair and equal treatment in the private sector of social life than in the public sector. Negro votes are far less useful in leading governments to pass laws that integrate public accommodations, insure fair employment practices and guarantee equal access to housing than they are in leading governments to eliminate government discrimination itself. Tuskegee's public accommodations and fair employment practices ordinances were the last major payoffs of Negro voting there, and Durham's city council has never acted on requests that it pass such ordinances. Part of the reason for this is that the ideology of free enterprise in the United States still resists government interference in the private sector. It is much easier for governments to make changes in areas that they already directly control than for them to change the scope of government and to begin to regulate something that had been unregulated before.

3. In attacking present discrimination in the private sector, votes will be more useful in eliminating such discrimination in public accommodations and employment than in housing. While votes have brought public accommodations and fair employment ordinances in Tuskegee, the prohibition of discrimination in the sale and rental of housing has scarcely become a public issue. In Durham, fair housing only became a public issue in 1967, four years after the peak of demands for action in fair employment and public accommodations. There are at least two reasons for this. One is that this has not been high on the list of Negro demands. Negro leaders have somehow been very slow in asking for fair housing. The other reason is that whites are probably more resistant to fair housing than to open public accommodations and fair employment. While integration of public accommodations affects whites only when they use them, and fair employment affects them only when they are at work, fair housing affects them when they are at home.

4. Within the public sector, votes more easily secure a fair and equal distribution of public goods than their integration. In Durham the school board has intransigently resisted school integration for a period of over ten years after the Brown decision. Negro votes were much more relevant to fair distribution of school facilities on a "separate but equal" basis than to integration of schools, where votes have been virtually useless. Also in public recreation, votes were not nearly so useful in integration as they were in equalizing the distribution of recreation facilities. White resistance to integration is obviously at the root of this. Securing fair distribution of facilities does not affect conditions for whites nearly so much as does integration of the facilities.

Whites do not have to be integrationists to tolerate or support fair distribution of public goods.

5. When public facilities are distributed as a result of bond issue elections, Negro votes have a better chance of insuring equal distribution than when facilities are distributed as a result of an independent decision by city officials. This has been argued at greater length above,[3] but the point was that issues are more salient in bond elections than in candidate elections, and that bond issue proponents are somewhat more vulnerable to the demands of Negro leaders for concessions in return for support than are candidates themselves. Consequently it is easier to make the fair distribution of a particular facility or service contingent on voting support when that facility or service is the sole issue of an election, than when it is buried among other issues or when it cannot be tied to any single election.

6. Votes are less useful where elected officials do not have direct responsibility for policy than where they do. School policy in Durham is made by a board which is appointed by the city council, but the city council for the most part washes its hands of any responsibility for school policy even though it indirectly controls it through its appointments. The same is true of public housing policy. When elected officials can say that resolution of a grievance is not in their hands, they more easily ignore the pressures of Negro votes than when they have a direct responsibility for policy in a given area. This is an effective excuse for inaction.

7. Negro votes more easily secure an incremental adjustment in existing policies than a totally new program. For example, Negro votes bring a fairer distribution of expenditures in an ongoing program, like placing streetlights and traffic signs on all corners, more easily than Negro votes bring a whole new program, like paving of all streets at city expense when this has been a private responsibility. To put it another way, Negro votes can secure pavement of streets more easily in Negro areas in a city like Tuskegee where city policy is to do this in all areas than in a city like Durham where the city does not provide this as a free service for anyone.

8. The less salient a policy change is, and the less visible it is to the public eye, the more influence Negroes (or other groups) can have on it through voting (or any other political resource). In a similar vein, Harry Eckstein has pointed out that the influence of groups is enhanced by the absence of high public interest in an area of policy, by extensive agreement about basic political issues, and by concern with narrowly

[3] See pp. 45, 58-64, 71-75, 77.

defined technical policies.[4] He argues that the influence of groups is greatest where it "matters the least."[5]

The underlying rationale of this hypothesis is the contention that when the general public or other groups are not watching, there is a freer rein for group influence. I expect that public officials would like to please groups and gain their support by meeting demands whenever doing so involves political gains without political costs. One reason why officials decline to meet demands is that they may feel that doing so will alienate the public or other groups whose support they may need. When issues are low in visibility or salience, group influence will correspondingly be increased because the public and other interested groups are less likely to be aware or concerned.

In this regard, an illustrative concrete contrast might be drawn between the success of Negro votes in securing better parks and recreational facilities in Negro areas and the repeated failures of Negro votes to secure school integration. The latter is a much more visible issue for the community as a whole. It is also far more salient, in that a great many people care a great deal about it and vigorously disapprove of action to integrate. When opponents of Negro demands are both concerned and aware that their preferences are being threatened, they are more likely to mobilize their opposition than when they are less concerned and aware. A Negro voting minority will not likely be able to prevail over a concerned white voting majority.

9. The final hypothesis in this section will propose three categories of policy which are ordered along a dimension of the crudeness or subtlety of the kinds of discrimination being attacked by Negro votes. Some forms of discrimination and mistreatment Negroes have suffered are cruder and more patently offensive than others. I hypothesize that the crudest forms will be least resistant to Negro voting strength, while the subtlest forms will be most resistant. As an example of the category that is crudest and least resistant to Negro voting, in one Mississippi county I visited, the road grader that regularly smooths the county's unpaved roads would pick up the blade when going through Negro residential areas! Practices like this, along with the kinds of police brutality designed to keep Negroes from getting "uppity," are especially wanton and malicious. They involve no savings or objective benefit to the white community. White officials would have difficulty acknowledging such activity, let alone defending it, particularly in the face of the incentive of Negro votes.

[4] *Pressure Group Politics* (Stanford, California: Stanford University Press, 1960), pp. 155-56.
[5] *Ibid.*, p. 157.

A second category, slightly more resistant to the effects of Negro voting, includes governmental decisions which also involve obvious considerations of fairness, but the difference between this category and the first is that decisions in this one may involve some kind of 'cost' to the white community. For example, impartiality is perhaps the most fundamental aspect of justice, but Negroes have been discriminated against in courts for years. Equal distribution of public services is closely related to democratic values of equal rights, but Negroes have been given inferior services for years as well. In both these cases, fair treatment of Negroes involves somewhat more cost to the community than cessation of brutality, or lowering the blade on the grader, in that white defendants may be more likely to lose civil suits or be convicted, or in that the community will have to pay for the same services in Negro districts that it does in others.

The third and last category, most resistant to Negro voting, is one in which the standards of equality and fairness are more subtle, though no less real. It includes integration of public or private facilities, wherein separate facilities are not obviously inherently unequal, and all activity in the private sector, wherein there are powerful elements of American political tradition which restrict the legitimacy with which the government can regulate the private sector of social life. This category also includes the elimination of the effects of past discrimination, wherein apparently special treatment *for* Negroes is necessary. The reasons that these goals will be more resistant to the power of the Negro vote, other things being equal, is that public officials and candidates will have a larger and more articulate clientele defending the status quo, and that they will find it less difficult to justify to themselves and to others that the status quo is defensible.

THE EFFECTS OF THE NATURE OF THE WHITE AND NEGRO ELECTORATES

Probably the most superficially plausible hypothesis we could propose about the impact of Negro voting is that the higher the proportion of the electorate Negro, the greater the payoffs of Negro voting will be. Yet this is obviously not always the case. Since the 1950's Tuskegee has had a higher proportion of its electorate Negro than Durham can ever expect to have, but the payoffs in Tuskegee were virtually nil until 1964, while Durham Negroes had enjoyed at least some gains as a result of their voting. How can this phenomenon be accounted for?

A large part of the answer lies in the attitudes and voting behavior of the remainder of the electorate. One of the clearest relationships to come out of previous research on southern racial politics is that "as the proportion of Negroes in southern communities increases, so do the racial anxieties and fears of southern whites."[6] The more Negroes there are in a given area, the more the whites will feel threatened by them. The more Negroes there are, the harder they will be to control, and consequently the more they are repressed by whites. This is why the states of the deep South have traditionally been more adamant on the race question; their Negro population is larger and demands more effort to control. This is also why 'black belt' areas of all the southern states are the most anti-Negro. They have the heaviest Negro concentration and in some cases Negro population majorities.[7] Such heavy concentrations of Negroes are a threat to white supremacy and help to produce some of the most rabid of white supremacists.

Since there is a very large majority of Negroes in Tuskegee, but only a sizeable minority in Durham, naturally Tuskegee whites would be more afraid of Negro political power and more resistant to the political demands of Negroes than Durham whites. While there is no direct evidence on this difference, the behavior of Tuskegee's *ancien régime* provides indirect support for the assertion.

But do the facts support the implausible argument that the smaller the size of the Negro electorate, the greater the payoffs from voting (ignoring Negro voting majorities)? No. This does not follow. All of the available evidence tells us that white anxiety is associated with the Negro proportion of the population, not of the electorate. There is no direct evidence that, in a community with a given Negro population proportion, white anxieties will vary with Negro registration or voting. One ironic possibility is that once whites discover how little Negro voting changes life styles of Negroes *or* whites, they will be *less* fearful of Negro "domination"! The reason that a large Negro voting minority in Tuskegee achieved less than a smaller one did in Durham is not because the one was large and the other was small. Rather it was largely due to the fact that Tuskegee is in a black belt area, has a Negro population majority and all of the white political insecurity that goes along with such a situation, and due to the fact that Durham has a Negro population minority and has been less afraid of what Negroes in politics

[6] Donald R. Matthews and James W. Prothro, *Negroes and the New Southern Politics* (New York: Harcourt, Brace and World, Inc., 1966), p. 117. See footnote 11 on the same page for further literature on the topic.
[7] The term "black belt" derives not from the high concentration of Negroes in these areas, but rather from the black soil there. The presence of many Negroes in the black belt is not coincidental, however, in that plantation culture flourished on the good, black soil, and Negro slaves were brought in to provide labor for the plantations.

could do. If the Durham whites who first allowed unrestricted Negro political participation years ago told themselves that doing so would not make much difference, this research has proven them correct.

The seeming paradoxes of the above account can be resolved by the following hypotheses. In any given community, with a given degree of white hostility, the benefits of Negro voting will be directly related to the size of the Negro electorate. However, communities with larger Negro populations have potentially larger Negro electorates, and as I pointed out above, the larger the Negro population proportion, the more anxious and repressive the whites. Thus when we compare different communities, rather than comparing times in one community, we find that the places with large Negro voting minorities are likely to have large Negro population minorities, or even majorities. Consequently the advantage of a larger Negro electorate may be counter-balanced by a more resistant white population. This accounts well for the fact that 45 percent of the votes in Tuskegee did not bring the gains that 25 or 30 percent did in Durham. Nevertheless, having 45 percent of the votes in Tuskegee is still worth more than having 30 percent *in that city,* even though 30 percent in Durham is worth more than 45 percent in Tuskegee. Where white resistance remains constant, Negro votes are directly related to payoffs.

If we assume that federal law has guaranteed the right to vote of all southern Negroes, and that the percent of eligible Negroes registered is relatively uniform over the whole region, we might expect a curvilinear relationship between percent of the electorate Negro and payoffs of voting. Up to about 30 percent of the electorate Negro the relationship would be positive because the threshold of white resistance seems to be 30 percent of the population Negro.[8] Between 30 and 50 percent of the electorate Negro, the relationship might become neutral or negative, because white resistance will be higher in communities with larger Negro population bases. Beyond 50 percent of the electorate Negro the relationship will again become positive, because, as Tuskegee illustrates, a Negro voting majority can overcome a lot of white resistance.

The above treatment helps us account for why fewer votes brought more gains in Durham than Tuskegee, by depending on differences in white attitudes between the two communities. Further analysis may be

[8] Matthews and Prothro observe that there seems to be a critical point at about 30 percent of the population Negro where white hostility to Negro political participation becomes severe. Perhaps resistance to other political demands of Negroes becomes severe at approximately the same point. See their "Social and Economic Factors and Negro Voter Registration in the South," *American Political Science Review,* LVII (1963), p. 29.

useful in accounting for variations in the responsiveness to Negro votes at a given level of white resistance to Negro rights and privileges, as well as at different levels of resistance. At any level of hostility to Negroes, that hostility may be more or less 'salient' to whites. That is to say that it may be a more or less dominant consideration in their voting. When the salience of race is high, we may expect that whites are highly cohesive in voting against Negroes or voting against candidates supported by Negroes. When the salience of race is low, whites will be less cohesive, and split on other issues or on personalities. The more salient race is to whites, the more responsive they are to racial dimensions of campaigns. If they are anti-Negro, they are more likely to respond to anti-Negro appeals by candidates and their supporters. In this sense, then, race may be more salient to whites in Tuskegee than in Durham. This would help account for the fact that whites in Tuskegee were always successful in resisting Negro demands in the face of a very large Negro minority of the voters. I hypothesize that the greater the Negro proportion of a population, the greater the salience of race to white voters.

These matters regarding the electoral environment can be viewed from the candidates' viewpoint as well. What Negro votes do from this perspective is to change and complicate incentives for candidates. Perhaps the safest incentive for any candidate to follow is to take the majority's position, but as Robert Dahl has shown, this is no guarantee of victory.[9] Dahl shows that a candidate favoring the minority position on all of three issues can win anyway. In fact if each alternative he favors is supported by only 25 percent of the voters, he can still win by as much as 75 percent of the vote if the minorities do not overlap and if they all vote cohesively for him. We know that the Negro minority in Durham is highly cohesive, and as such it provides a realistic and compelling incentive. The more cohesive and maneuverable those votes are, the more realistic and compelling the incentive.

Even so, candidates in Durham and *ancien régime* Tuskegee have remained strikingly cool in the face of such incentives. They have hardly fallen over themselves to earn Negro support. Perhaps they feel that soliciting Negro votes will make race more salient to white voters. Perhaps they fear that responding to Negro demands will lead their opponents to intensify the race issue. The cry of "Nigger" is all too familiar in Southern politics. Occasionally a candidate for Durham city council will crudely court the backlash, but in recent years at least, this tactic has not been very profitable. On the other hand, many candidates are

[9] *Preface to Democratic Theory* (Chicago: University of Chicago Press, 1956), p. 128.

not above making it clear that their opponents are receiving the Negro vote. Most recently in 1967 the incumbent mayor campaigned with ads proclaiming "I will not get the bloc vote!" He did point out that he had always received it before and that his administrations had been based on fairness for all, but "Fairness has not been enough!" He won by over 2,000 votes out of almost 17,000 cast.

Still the kiss of death treatment does not insure victory in Durham. One other candidate in the same election who also proclaimed that he did not have the bloc vote lost by over 1,000 votes. States rights and Ku Klux Klan candidates have lost very badly, and have not even been serious contenders in Durham in recent years.

Perhaps the moral is that politicians are not very great risk takers. Even when changes seem to have widespread support, politicians do not always feel called upon to respond. As V. O. Key has said, "The opinion context, therefore, may be regarded as a negative factor; it fixes the limitations within which action may be taken but does not assure that action will be taken."[10] Even in Durham there is hardly such a permissive consensus among whites as to permit some of the concessions I cited as most resistant to Negro voting without substantial risk to elected officials. Even so, Durham's officials have been particularly cautious, and they have not even done all of those things that they could without risking white support. In *ancien régime* Tuskegee, elected officials were probably as adamant in the face of Negro demands as was the white public, yet it is hard to imagine that the officials could not have solicited Negro votes by making some low visibility concessions. The point is that the democratic process does not guarantee that governments will meet as many of the needs of a minority as the majority will tolerate.

THE IMPACT OF NEGRO LEADERSHIP

I have argued at several points in chapter IV that public officials are not always very imaginative in thinking of ways to solicit votes or mobilize support from population groupings, and that the prospects of Negro votes gaining advantages for Negroes are enhanced if voters or leaders ask for them. If gains do not automatically result from Negro votes, the votes must be supplemented with demands, requests or pressure, whichever may be more appropriate. The very existence of a sizeable group of Negro voters in Durham and Tuskegee is the remarkable achievement of Negro leadership and organization in those cities. Similarly, school integration in both cities resulted from court

[10] *Public Opinion and American Democracy* (New York: Alfred A. Knopf, 1961), p. 424.

suits initiated by Negro leaders. Yet it does not appear that the leaders of the DCNA and MCDC have been quite so aggressive in demanding concessions in return for voting support as they have been in registering and mobilizing votes and in going to court. Perhaps this is simply a reflection of their style, but they do not for the most part seem to have risked losing entree with public officials because they asked for too much. Just how much bargaining has gone on between the Negro organizations' leaders and candidates seeking their support is not clear, but bargaining and threats seem to have played a very minor role.

Since the findings indicate that votes have not been a very useful resource for Negroes who compose a minority of an electorate, one wonders whether this was because of inherent limitations of the vote or because of failures on the part of Negro leaders to follow up their voting strength with demands and 'pressure.' Raising this question is to indulge in a little Monday morning quarterbacking, but given the importance of the question this seems forgivable. In chapter IV I contrasted two strategies by which Negro voting minorities could try to get the maximum impact out of their endorsements.[11] There the question was whether to use the endorsement merely to respond to existing differences between candidates with a minimal risk of making it a kiss of death, or to use the endorsement to try to improve the alternatives but thereby increase the risk of a kiss of death. Just as it is possible for heavy-handedness in trying to improve alternatives to backfire, heavy handedness in making demands may backfire and eliminate whatever entree votes had brought.

We must remember that a minority of votes cannot be used to force concessions unless the issues, personalities or other loyalties that divide the majority of voters are more enduring than those voters' opposition to concessions to the minority, unless victory means more to a candidate than maintaining the status quo, and unless the demands have enough legitimacy to allow candidates who make them to remain viable with the remainder of the voters. Votes are not useful to secure what a majority is unwilling to concede. Neither are they useful to secure what none of the candidates with a realistic chance of winning consider legitimate concessions. Given white attitudes towards race, this by itself will cut down the possible gains to be secured by Negro votes. One of the major changes of the 1950's and 1960's is that full and equal citizenship for Negroes has taken on considerably more legitimacy among both candidates for office and white publics than it had before. Thus the prospects for the successful use of Negro voting to secure

[11] Pp. 42-48.

gains for Negroes have improved in the same period. Even so, action in the private sector, action to integrate and action to eliminate the effects of past discrimination still do not have the kind of legitimacy in many areas to make them issues that a minority of Negro votes can do much about. "Fairness" and "equal distribution" have a relatively high legitimacy, and consequently these are areas where Negro votes have the greatest prospect of success. If school integration has low legitimacy among candidates and white voters, leaders of a Negro minority will waste their time in trying to use votes to gain it. Litigation is demonstrably more useful. The most promising thing leaders of a Negro minority can do is to articulate grievances over as many examples of unfairness and injustice as they can find in the public sector, and to make their voting support contingent on resolution of these grievances. Issues should be defined in terms of simple standards of fairness, justice and equality whenever possible, and the unfairness of any situation should be played up.

The really striking gains of Durham's Negro minority have come through resources other than votes. Litigation brought school integration. Demonstrations and boycotts have brought changes in the private sector. The vote failed in these areas, but there is little that Negro leaders could have done to bring about these gains through voting.

The safest strategy for leaders of a Negro voting minority to use is to support the candidates who give the greatest evidence of fairmindedness and willingness to abide by basic standards of justice and equality. But this is not enough. This must be supplemented with a vigilance that identifies and records all failures to treat Negroes fairly. All too often officials will treat Negroes unfairly when they can get away with it. If Negro leaders 'catch' them in each instance, and cast each grievance in terms of fairness, justice and equal treatment, officials will find it hard to maintain unfair practices, and easier to make the adjustment with impunity from the white majority. Where Negroes are mistreated, they cannot be adequately represented and led by Negroes who do no more than respond to racial dimensions or dimensions of unfairness and injustice of those issues that happen to come up. They and their supporting Negro organizations must solicit information about all grievances, articulate them and demand change. A lot of injustice goes on as long as it is ignored. If Negro leaders ignore it, it is likely to continue. If they do not ignore it, if they seek it out, Negro votes can be important incentives for officials to respond with fairness and justice. Votes do not guarantee even basic standards of fairness and justice, but they can add to the costs of violating those standards, and add to the incentives for obeying them. Even so, the power of votes to do so is not much greater than the sensitivity of candidates to the standards, but Negro votes can make candidates more sensitive.

If I have been correct in arguing that the prospects that Negro votes will bring full and equal citizenship to Negroes is one of the more important questions for democratic theory and empirical political science, this book should be supplemented with further research on the topic. We need to investigate the effects of different sizes of voting minorities on resulting gains. We need to know the effects of Negro votes on policy when those votes are not mobilized into cohesive and maneuverable blocs, and when they are not led by economically secure middle class Negroes. What is the impact of Negro voting in the North? What is the impact of Negro voting in communities where voters and leaders have different values and political styles from those in Durham and Tuskegee? What are the payoffs of Negro voting in completely rural areas and in the nation's great metropolitan areas? More generally, what is the power of the votes of other minority groups to secure concessions for them?

THE ROLE OF THE VOTE IN THE QUEST FOR EQUALITY

Let us return to the key question with which the book began. To what extent has the evidence supported the contention that votes protect the rights of minorities in a democracy? The conclusion is not encouraging. Under very unfavorable circumstances like those of *ancien régime* Tuskegee, a substantial body of votes left Negroes disadvantaged on almost every dimension on which Negroes anywhere in the United States were disadvantaged. The absence of the worst kinds of police harassment there may be in part attributable to the vote, but the fact that some Negroes there had earned educations and desirable jobs through Tuskegee Institute and the Veterans Administration Hospital certainly was not. Otherwise, Tuskegee Negroes suffered the full range of public and private discrimination. Durham is a less unfavorable situation to begin with and the vote has not left Negroes so shortchanged there as it did in Tuskegee before Negroes became a majority. But Negroes in Durham are still reminding observers that their problems are by no means solved. Only sometimes does this lack of resolution of their problems imply that important whites or Negroes have been negligent. Only sometimes could these difficulties have been resolved by more aggressiveness on the part of Negro leaders or more responsiveness on the part of whites.

The vote is a far more potent instrument for achieving legal justice than social justice. The gains I have found to be most susceptible to Negro voting have consistently been those which most clearly involved fair and just administration of existing laws. Social justice, however, demands more than this. It often demands changes in existing laws. For example, when discriminating against Negroes in hiring is legal, social justice may demand legislation to make such discrimination illegal. With few exceptions the vote has failed Durham and Tuskegee Negroes when they sought to change the law in order to eliminate existing discrimination. I have argued that, because of the effects of past discrimination, Negroes do not have equal opportunity for personal, social and economic advancement even when existing discrimination is eliminated. If social justice demands the eradication of the effects of past discrimination, the vote is even less useful.

These observations have significant implications for democratic theory. Votes are a key resource in a democracy in that they are very widely distributed, and in that all decisions are ultimately subject to the influence of votes. Even the Constitution itself ultimately rests on votes. Votes are not a key resource, however, in the sense that they might be expected to equalize opportunities for advancement or to bring social justice. Universal suffrage is perfectly consistent with a highly stratified society which does not offer an equal chance for every citizen to pursue life, liberty and happiness. Durham is an excellent example of this.

Insofar as democracy involves majority rule, the findings are perfectly congruent with what democratic theory would lead us to expect. White voting majorities have prevailed consistently over Negro minorities in both Durham and Tuskegee. In Tuskegee a Negro voting majority has prevailed over a white minority. This is not surprising, but the issue of minority rights is somewhat more complex. Votes do help protect legal rights even though they do not guarantee them. The minority rights which votes do most to protect are those which are either already embedded in law or those which are so firmly a part of the political culture that they have substantial support from that source. Votes do not seem to do much to insure protection of the rights of equal opportunity for personal advancement.

The findings of this book do not support Rousseauian notions that full participation in a democracy will bring about the achievement of the best interests of all citizens either in the form of a general will or in the form of some automatic approximation of a common denominator of preferences. It makes more sense, I think, to view the democratic process as one in which elites compete for mass support in terms which are defined by what is legitimate in the political culture and by the goals and appeals of the elites themselves.[12] Votes of mass publics are important in that they can determine which elites will win public office and in that they provide incentives for the elites to make more popular appeals which will meet the demands and interests of voting groups. When the demands of minorities have a high legitimacy in a given society, it is easy for elites to make appropriate concessions without endangering their support from other segments. In Durham and Tuskegee, fair and equitable administration of the laws has a relatively high legitimacy. Consequently votes have been useful there for such ends. Programs that would eliminate social inequalities and equalize life chances among Negroes and whites do not have such high legitimacy in either city. This is part of the reason that candidates there do not appeal for Negro votes on this basis.

Thus the formal mechanisms of democracy do not assure much more than that elites will have incentives to meet demands that do not conflict with the values of the elites and of the majority of the voters. The prospects that votes will help eliminate basic inequalities in the life chances of Negroes are contingent on the degree to which appropriate programs fit within the value structure of elites and voting majorities.

Does this mean that because such programs do not have high legitimacy in the settings studied here, the Negro can hope to gain no more than he can achieve through voting? The answer is almost certainly no, although the next steps are not clear. In the past fifteen years Negroes have depended heavily for their gains on two resources: litigation and direct action. Schools were integrated in both Durham and Tuskegee as a result of court action. Negro jurors in Macon County were the result of litigation. Integration of lunch counters in Durham was the result of sit-ins and boycotts. Concessions in fair employment and integration of numerous public accommodations in Durham were the result of demonstrations and marches.

Ironically, it may be that at this point the Negro is more dependent on voting strength than he was ten years ago before some of the above concessions had been gained. Litigation is no longer so useful. When local practices were in conflict with Federal Law, Negroes had legality on their side. This is now much less often the case. Local practices are now for the most part in tune with local and Federal law. The sorts of concessions the Negro needs most now are changes in law, and these are no longer forthcoming in the courts. Another problem is

[12] See Joseph A. Schumpeter, *Capitalism, Socialism and Democracy* (3rd ed., New York: Harper and Row, Publishers, 1950), pt. IV.

that the courses of action that will resolve racial inequality are not so clear as they were when schools and public accommodations were segregated and when it was legal to discriminate against Negroes in hiring. Open housing is one easily identifiable goal, but no one is under the illusion that the elimination of discrimination in housing will eliminate racial inequality.

Protests in the form of marches on city hall and the threat of violence have been used by Durham Negroes to buttress their demands as recently as summer 1967. While the record is not yet complete, it does appear that the protests have brought some concessions in public housing policy and city hiring policy. James Wilson has observed that "protest action is best suited to situations in which the goal sought is defensive, specific, of a welfare character, relevant to the wants of the Negro rank-and-file, and has a specific target."[13] Writing in 1961, Wilson points out that such goals are more common in the South than in the North. Now that some of the more specific goals of the civil rights movement have been attained in the South, that region is more like the North in that Negro needs and demands are no longer so specific and in that they do not so clearly have specific targets.

Whether riots and violence will bring positive gains is not clear, nor is it clear that riots are being used as a tactic to secure concessions. One thing that they clearly do is to call attention to the overwhelming problems of American Negroes, particularly those in ghettos, in an era in which most of the primary goals of the civil rights movement have been achieved. The threat of violence can make public officials more responsive to Negro demands, as I think it has in Durham, although it can also make public officials more rigidly resistant to Negro goals.

The real problem is much deeper than these tactical considerations imply. The tragedy of American racial history is that it has left the Negro with more problems than men of good-will are able to solve. Votes, litigation and even the threat of violence are useful because they can influence the behavior of elected policy-makers. The most frustrating problem of the American Negro in politics is that even if elected policy-makers were totally responsive to Negro demands, it is not at all clear that they have it in their power to eliminate the inequality with which three and a half centuries of discrimination have saddled the American Negro.

---

[13] "The Strategy of Protest: Problems of Negro Civic Action," *Journal of Conflict Resolution*, V (1961), pp. 291-303, reprinted in Harry A. Bailey, Jr., ed., *Negro Politics in America* (Columbus, O.: Charles E. Merrill Books, Inc., 1967), p. 63.

Index

Printed in U.S.A.